The literal hell of customer support jobs

First edition

Alessandra Della Rocca

2024

Disclaimer

This book is a work of fiction. Any resemblance to actual persons, living or deceased, or to actual businesses, companies, events, or locations is entirely coincidental and unintentional. While certain elements may be inspired by real-life experiences or historical events, the characters, settings, and occurrences presented in this story are products of the author's imagination.

This book is intended for entertainment purposes only. The author has made every effort to avoid depicting any real-life individuals or organizations. Any similarities that may be perceived are purely coincidental.

Table of content

Chapter 1: Intro

I feel like no one prepared me for adulthood. More specifically, how fast it arrived. One minute, I was in high school, and the next, I was doing taxes. Born and raised in Italy, I learned English through the Disney Channel and the Jonas Brothers' songs. I always knew this skill would come in handy one day. I never saw a future for me in Italy. There aren't many job opportunities, studying is complex, and the salary I would be getting is way too low to be worth the effort.

On top of that, I come from a small village in the south of Italy. There are more sheeps than people, though I sometimes count them together. The people my age have been unemployed for as long as I can remember. They have qualifications but need opportunities to prove themselves. Unfortunately, the trees from the local farms grow a handful of juicy fruits but not money. My career choices are limited; I can watch over the sheep or the babies of those watching the sheep. I quickly realised the grass was greener elsewhere, but I didn't know where exactly.

I knew that speaking English was an advantage. I was happy to learn that specific jobs were looking for Italian and

English speakers like me. Bilingual people are especially wanted for customer support jobs. I think I know the job and what it entails. I sometimes get people on the phone to fix the Internet when my router is down. This can't be hard. There is a need in the market for workers like me to be able to communicate with customers in Italian while being given directions in English. I like to think of it as the bridge between two worlds. It's a rewarding feeling. I started to do some research. There are a lot of companies looking for customer support agents. Their websites have videos of their teams playing ping pong in an office. There are rooms with televisions, a smoothie bar... The locations for these positions are also quite diverse: in Portugal or the Philippines, places with a lot of potential to sip cocktails on the beach after work. Most of the job offers are from American companies. There are big names that I and everybody else know. I find the idea of working for them impressive. I imagine situations where I introduce myself to people at a party, saying I work for a worldwide tech leader. I find it class. I like to be associated with big names. It makes me feel taller in the world.

Applying means that I have to leave Italy to go and work these jobs. Neither I nor my tarot reader see a professional future for me in this country. I don't really mind packing up and going. The comfort of an office job when the wind doesn't blow up in my face is something I would consider, and the idea of working as a support agent quickly became acceptable to me. Immigrating to a new country is a cultural experience I need to do now that I'm young and full of energy. I will make friends worldwide and have valuable experiences and big company names to add to my resume. I will improve my English and travel the world at the same time. This feels like a no-brainer: It's the perfect deal for me.

The job requirements aren't high. Customer support is an entry-level job requiring me to speak English and my mother tongue fluently. I have to excel both in writing and speaking. I also need good communication skills, and I can count on my background as a waitress for that. I was especially interested in listening to interviews of the people working in these companies. I've seen a video of a woman saying she started as a support agent and became the head of human resources years later. I find this to be inspiring and motivating. With a million advertisements all over the Internet and a real need for workers, I am confident that I can make this work for me. I will reach the top of corporations, starting at the bottom of the ladder. My success story is going to be like no other. I will exceed expectations, work harder than anyone else, and become a businesswoman overseas, making everyone in my hometown jealous. This is the beginning of my story, and I can't wait to write the next chapter.

Chapter 2: Purple

The quest for customer support jobs must be done somewhere other than Italy. I have to be out there to get the opportunities I want. I noticed that big European cities tend to have many available customer support positions. It was now up to me to decide where to go. I honestly would go anywhere; I want to start this adventure.

I'm unsure if my phone sensed my desperation or was actively listening to me, but the answer to my prayers came in the form of an Instagram ad the next day.

'You want to start a career in the video game industry?' it said.

Hell, yeah. I find this to be exciting. I've always been a fan of video games. This is mind-blowing. I cannot believe this is an actual ad. Working in the video game industry is the most appealing offer I could come across. I follow the link in the ad, and I'm redirected to an application form. I learned that the location for this job is in Amsterdam. It will be cold, but it's such a cute city that I don't care. I'm already liking it. They're asking about my age, what languages I can speak, my diplomas, and my favourite video games. This question alone is enough to determine that I want to spend the rest of my life in this company. Do they really want to know what I'm playing? This is so cool. I can hardly describe how hyped I am. The following day, I received a message from the recruiter, Jon. He says he will meet up with me in a video conference in a few days. I'm jumping around in my apartment. The hours are long, and the days pass slowly until the moment finally arrives. I'm connecting to the call. I turn on my webcam, and he is there. I'd say he's 30 and has brown hair, glasses, and a nice shirt. He looks like a geek who turned himself into a businessman. I feel an instant connection. He asks questions about myself. I did well during this part of the interview since I'm my own favourite topic. He continues by introducing the company Purple. He says it's a company that provides customer support for brands like video games and electronics. In a nutshell, they're not the brand itself, but they're handling the customer support part of a brand for them. That makes sense since support is complicated to put in place. He also told me what he expected from me, which was to take calls and answer emails on behalf of the company. I will be contacted by customers who need support on a specific product. Now comes the second part of the interview. He asks about the company. I don't know what to say. To be honest, I didn't do any research and didn't know that I should. He asks again, and I'm struggling to phrase any answer. I can't find my words, so I repeat myself and stutter. I'm getting warm. The feeling of embarrassment takes over, and I'm losing control of the interview. I'm visibly lost. I have phases in which I open my mouth but do not speak. It's like I forgot the lyrics to a song

I'm performing on stage. He continues to ask various questions about the company. I don't know if he can't take a hint, tries to give me a 5th chance or takes an evil pleasure in humiliating me a bit more every time he questions my knowledge of the company. I'm trying to keep what's left of my dignity to do a discreet Google search so I can get out of this situation. He knows I'm typing something on Google because he asks me to stop. What's left of my dignity just dissolved into thin air.

I am exhausted. This part lasted 8 minutes, but it felt like 8 hours of being backed into a corner and repeatedly beat with my own stupidity.

At last, he asks: 'Did you … not do any research about the company?'.

He raises an eyebrow, and his tone becomes condescending. It was obvious that I did not and obvious that he figured this out a while ago. Why did he choose to address it only now? It didn't matter. I dug myself too deep to get out of this mess; I had no choice but to bury myself so I could end my misery. This went on for too long.

'No,' I say coldly and calmly.

I'm entirely changing my behaviour. I'm giving up. He can tell. I'm losing the pose and fall back on my chair like a teenager.

—' So why did you apply for this job exactly?' he asks.

—' I found the Instagram ad, and I thought it was cool.' I answer.

—' So, you applied for this job randomly. Is that what you're saying?'

—' Yeah.'

I suppose recruiters aren't used to honesty, but seriously, are they expecting each applicant to have done hours of investigation before their interview? Was I supposed to go through their Wikipedia page? Add their HR on LinkedIn? Sample the coffee they use in the office? In the corporate world, the answer to all of these questions is, unfortunately, yes. I am too young and not prepared enough for this. I want it to end. We finish the interview awkwardly. We both want to hang up. He tells me he'll be in touch. I nod and close my laptop. I run to my bed and cover my head with a pillow. I scream internally. I missed my chance with an incredible company. I should've known better and prepared for the interview. I couldn't know. I could've known. I don't know what to think anymore. I just know that I killed my chances.

The next morning, I received the most unexpected email. It was Jon: I got the job. I take a few seconds to make sure I read the email correctly. It does say that I got the job. I sit on the couch and take a moment to process the information. And I scream. I'm exploding with joy. With some divine intervention, they decided to hire me after the worst interview they had ever had with a candidate. Because I'm naive, I don't see this as a huge red flag, meaning I got the job because no one else applied. It means that even though I was a terrible candidate, they have no one else to turn to and are forced to contract my terribly unprepared self. I innocently believed that they saw something in me, that my honesty paid, and that my personality would get me far in the company.

I bought a one-way ticket to Amsterdam and booked temporary accommodation close to the office for a month. I will be living there until I find something permanent. Upon arriving, I felt the change in temperature. This isn't the south of Italy anymore. Regardless, I'm ready to start working.

This is my first day. I walk into the office. It is located on the 5th floor of a shopping centre. Beneath us are all the shops and restaurants, but we can't hear a thing. The walls are soundproof. I arrived, but I'm not sure if I'm the first. The office is quiet; there's a woman sitting on a couch. She looks just as lost as me. She's one of the candidates, my new colleague. She introduced herself: 'I'm Sophia'. She seems bored and exhausted already. She's in her 30s, and she already knows she won't last long here. She doesn't need to work, she says. Her brother-in-law is super rich, and she lives with him. I've always been fascinated by people who don't actually need to work but do it anyway as a hobby, to pass the time, an experiment to see how the rest of the world makes a living. The third candidate arrives. He's a tall and skinny man in his mid-30s as well. He's well dressed, with a nice suit, a scarf, and a watch. I wonder if he is here for the interview or has already got the job. I can't understand the need to dress up as nicely to stay in a small office for 8 hours. But then he explains. As we exchange casualties, he tells me about his professional path. He opened up a company, was CEO for a few years and has impressive diplomas in marketing. Sophia adds that she has a law diploma and has worked for big companies in Ireland, but she is not impressed by this one. I'm pretty intimidated. These are my colleagues? They're way too qualified to be doing this. How is it that I just left high school and now have the same pay rate as a competent CEO?

A new woman walks in. Her name is Rose. She's smiling ear to ear and has a calm voice. She says she is our manager. She gives us a tour of the office so we know where to make coffee and, most importantly, where to wash our mugs after use. It's plastered pretty much everywhere that we have to wash our mugs. She goes up to people to introduce them to us. Most of them are already working and are just waving their hands without looking away from their screen. *Great, we're going to be good friends.* She makes jokes about it, but rather than laugh with them, she laughs by herself. They don't bother to try. What a good impression. And then she takes us to our department. By department, I mean the corner of this open space where we're all going to be working. There are three other people there already, one guy who's apparently new as well. He's Danish and has the weirdest moustache I've ever seen. It's twirling, and it seems solid. I wondered if he put hair spray on it. I try to joke about it, but he looks at me dead seriously and does not reply. I'm unsure if he didn't find it funny, didn't understand it or just decided he would not like me. And to my left are the two most advanced agents this department has. They've both been working here for a few years and are keen on the product. This will come in handy later. They both seem super chill; the woman, Leah, has a lot of tattoos and blue hair. She looks like the most genuine person here, judging by her smile. She's not forcing it; she's happy to see new people. And the guy Cedric has long straight hair, beautifully straightened and tied up, an inexpressive face and a nice white shirt with long sleeves. I sit at my desk and find a cap with the company's name and an apple. *An apple.* The budget for this welcoming gift is out of this world. But I take it; it's my first time in an office, my first step in the corporate world, and gifts are another reason to be excited about this journey. Another man walks up to our desks once we're all installed and greets us with little to no enthusiasm. It's disturbing. His voice intonates correctly for a first greeting, but his face doesn't. It's like a table read for comedians just saying their lines out loud without actively acting them. He says his name is Brett, and he is our manager. I'm now confused. Is he the manager? Then who is Rose? Are they both our managers? I don't know it yet, but apparently, this happens quite a lot in the corporate world. It's never clear who's the manager. Some people, in fact, are not managers. They're just using the title because they're a supervisor reporting to the manager or a point of contact between agents and the manager. This sounds too long and complicated. The 'manager' title will do better. This also begins the weird and perpetuated corporate habit of finding a classier name for a job than what it actually is. I'm not a customer support agent; *I'm part of the customer experience team, and I'm an advisor.* Rose is not a 2nd supervisor with no power other than to report to her higher-up; *she is our manager.* And Brett is her manager. He wishes us good luck and walks away.

I create my account on my computer and connect with my colleagues. There are a few headphones in the office. Rose is showing them to us and asks us to try them on. She continues by saying we'll support the brand making them. This is not what I was told during the recruitment process. This is not video game support at all. Some office people support a video game company, but not us. I mind for a little while before I accept my faith and try to make the most of it. At the end of the day, we are asked to try the products. I connect one pair of headphones to my mobile and play one of my favourite artists. The sound is great, and I find it incredible to be paid to listen to music. This lasts an hour before we go home; the first day is over. *It isn't that bad,* I'm thinking. It is usually never on the first day.

On the second day, I start training for the product I'll be assisting. By training, I mean I'm given a bunch of PDFs to read, and I have to do some quizzes to make sure I understand the content of these documents. There are knowledgeable colleagues one meter away from me who could teach me, but this is how we're being trained. Support jobs will be fully explained through documents, presentations and games. This does not bother me initially, but after 8 hours of clicking through pages, I'm exhausted. I don't even read anymore; I click on 'Next' to get to the end of the document as quickly as possible. We're being fed too much information, some of which we'll never use. There's a 13-page PDF about how Bluetooth was created. How is this relevant to my job? I suppose it's good for culture, but it's the last thing I want to be reading at the end of my day. Surprisingly enough, we're being told very little about the job. All the documents talk about the products, the technology being used, and the company. There's nothing about the type of queries we'll receive, who the clients are and how to greet them when they call. The training feels unbalanced. I'd like to know more about my daily tasks and less about the history of Bluetooth. After one week, we finally get a glimpse of what the job will look like. My colleagues and I are following a schedule that we received via email. Despite having two managers in the office, I have to follow the directions of an email to know what to do during my day. The tasks are written as such:

9 a.m.: Get familiar with our website

10:00 a.m.: Read this PDF

10:30 a.m.: 30 minutes breaks

It's not clear to me if they intentionally don't want to overwhelm us, but most of the time, I'm trying to figure out what to do. I try not to be on my phone because I want to look professional, but my managers are washing their mugs too far away to see me. I imagine them doing that anyway because I barely see them around in the office. I spy on my colleagues to see what they do. They're clicking around their computer, not doing more than me. The rhythm of the training is strange. It goes really fast some days, and other days, we're just laying around in the office.

On the third day, I arrived at the office at the same time as Rose. I took the elevator with her. A man walked in. He's in his 40s, though he looks 60 already. He's a bit fat, and not a lot of hair remains on the top of his head. He looked at me, told me his name, and shook my hand. I did the same. He walked out once we reached the 5th floor. Rose looked at me with eyes wide open.

'That's the CEO!' she says with excitement.

Really? That man is the CEO? She looks starstruck as if we just met Tom Hanks. Isn't she taking the elevator with him every week? Apparently, someone important paying attention to us is a big deal here. He just shook my hand, though. He did not offer me a job as vice president.

I sit at my desk, greet my colleagues who are already here, and take off my coat. I start my computer when I hear someone's voice I don't recognise.

'Hey guys', I hear.

I lift my head to see a guy atop my computer screen. He asks if we're having fun. Rose follows him, laughing.

'Guys, this is Jerry!'. She introduced him to us.

'Hi Jerry', we politely reply.

She tells us that Jerry works here but is unsure what he does. He's just funny. They laugh together at this. I'm looking at my colleagues, not knowing how to react. I'm not sure who this guy is and why he wants to meet us. Also, is doing nothing an option? I'll take this job any day. He is probably a quality analyst or someone who works in HR. They are usually the ones who do the least. After 5 minutes of failed attempts to interact with us, he leaves the floor. I didn't mean to come across as cold. At this point, I'm not comfortable enough within this environment to know if I should let loose or keep my guard up. The job is different from what I was told it would be, so I stay vigilant to ensure no one else can trick me anymore.

I have started to handle real cases from customers. They're primarily lengthy emails describing a technical issue I'm unfamiliar with and don't know how to fix. I use some of my brain to develop common sense replies such as 'Turn off your device and then turn it back on'. I'm generally clueless as to what I should do or say. The resources I was given during the training covered broad scenarios but nothing in detail. I learn as I go that I have to categorise my cases. The technical issues need to be classified so as not to be mistaken for refunds. I'm curious as to why we're doing this because we never go back to these cases and don't even use this classification for metrics. But I do it anyway because I am told to do so and follow directions well. I also need to properly log the user's profile onto the system. A lot of back and forth happens during my first interactions. I have to ask a lot of questions because I have no idea what the customer is talking about, and I need all the information I can get to ask for help from the colleague next to me. It's difficult to pretend like I'm asking probing questions to get into specificities without revealing that I don't know what I'm talking about. If they report that their speaker isn't charging, I ask if they have electricity at home. Thankfully, it takes a while for most of these users to come back to me after I ask them the stupidest questions ever. It gives me time to brace myself before interacting with them another time. But the next day, I can be sure that they will still be here and waiting for me to solve their issue.

The most stressful part for me is the phone. I'm not handling calls well at all. I live in fear of hearing the phone ring. I have to answer and discuss something I barely know with someone who thinks I'm an expert. The calls are awkward. Neither the customer nor I know how to go about the conversation. It's like talking to a family member I haven't seen in years. We're supposed to speak, but we don't know about what. I get out of most calls with customers by saying I'll send them an email with steps to follow. Then, I copy and paste the steps from my colleague's notes, and I hope for the best.

Without noticing, a routine begins. I arrive at the office every morning, grab a mug and make myself a coffee. I turn on my computer and prepare to deal with the day's cases. I follow up with the cases from the day before, and each teaches me more about my job, the product I'm supporting and how to fix most problems. It gets easier by the day, and after a few weeks, I learn what I should've known since day one. Unfortunately for me and the customers who speak to me on a regular basis, the training provided by the company focuses more on the personal history of the CEO rather than the basic troubleshooting steps to solve a technical problem. I learn through trial and error and thank the users for their patience. Sometimes, they fix things on their own, and they tell me how they did it.

'Good news! I pressed that button for five seconds, and it worked!' they informed me ecstatically.

I make sure to write down any solution I come across to use later. After each reply I send, I get a new case from a new customer. I never know who I'm going to get. Whether it's someone who is a bit tech-savvy or someone who does not know how to turn on a computer. It is a contractual obligation not to make fun of these ones, but I can't really respect anyone who's struggling to take a screenshot of their computer screen. The worst ones take a picture of their screen with their phone, send it via email to themselves, and forward it to me. I'm lucky enough to review these beautiful photographs of their blurry screen with light reflecting on it. Getting all sorts of weird attachments in emails becomes part of the job. One user sends me a picture of their headset, which they put on a table next to magazines with an almost naked Christina Aguilera on the cover. I'm not sure why they decided to include the magazines in the shot and why they didn't think of cropping the picture before sending it to me. I don't mind a bit of Christina. The more contacts I get, the weirder humanity becomes to me. Some people call me with their baby crying in their arms, making the conversation impossible. Some people call me from their car, which ensures that the call is cut off every 5 minutes, making it a pleasant conversation. And while I can't say for certain that they're calling from the toilet, I suspect some customers to be guilty of that because of the amount of reverberation I can hear on the phone. Emails are different; it's tougher to get a clear picture of who's contacting me. Some write their email in a professional manner, with a greeting, a description of their problem and a polite formulation. Others write: 'DOES NOT WORK! HELP ASAP!!!'. I have to guess everything from these 5 words in caps, of course. I wonder why someone would write such an evasive email to begin with. Are they being held hostage? Was it the only thing they managed to write after snatching a mobile from one of the kidnappers to send a help message? The most concise messages usually come from the least patient customers who want their problem fixed in a second without giving away any information required to resolve their issue. I wish I could magically guess what they're talking about, but I'm not a psychic. I'm a customer support agent, and it's a lot less fun. I alternate between all these types of contacts until my shift ends and the time comes for me to wash my mug. I'm mentally absent. I'm not sure that 8 hours just passed even though I felt how long every minute was. I look at my colleagues before I leave the office, and I can't read a thing on their faces. It's almost as if we're all in autopilot mode. I don't have a feeling of accomplishment because I accomplished nothing. Most of the questions I'm being asked are left unanswered. I will have to do this tomorrow, too. And the day after, and the day after that.

In the open space, we can sometimes hear each other's calls. There are 6 of us working on the same product, and our desks are glued together in a rectangular shape. Three on each side. Leah is one of the advanced agents. She often takes calls in her sweet and calm voice. But today, the call is different. It lasts longer than usual, and she repeats herself a lot. After a while, she starts turning red, her eyes water. It contrasted with her blue hair, I thought. It's funny. But then I thought, it's not funny. This woman is in tears because someone is yelling at her on the phone on the other side of the world. Why isn't anybody moving? If this happened in a restaurant, surely a colleague would come to try to de-escalate the situation. Can anyone take over? Can anyone take the headset away from her, put it on their own head and continue the call? Right now, no one is paying attention. They all look briefly when her voice goes a bit louder than usual. But then they all go back to whatever they are doing. Clicks and keyboard sounds can be heard between the sobbing of this poor colleague of mine. And yet she continues. I can barely hear it in her voice that she's about to cry. She's very poised. She slightly raised her voice, exasperated, but I couldn't tell she was angry or exhausted if I wasn't seeing her. Her face reads, 'I'm questioning my whole life and what I'm doing here', but her voice continues to have a proper tone to address the customer. That is the first time I've ever seen someone with such composure dealing with a delicate situation. Is it a standard practice for agents to switch off emotions during phone calls? I know that the people we're calling to solve issues are known to be rude and unhelpful, but this one is my colleague. I met this woman. She's nice to me. We are laughing together every day. And now she's ice-cold and melting at the same time. How bizarre. As my concern grows, I do my best to listen to the call so I understand what's the matter. From what I can gather, it seems like the customer is unhappy with the resolution she's giving him. He wants us to send him a new headset for free because the previous one he purchased broke. He's out of the warranty period, so we cannot process this request. She's following Purple's guidelines and is doing her job correctly. That call ends with her telling the customer that they can call again, they'll still get her on the phone, and she'll give the same answer. She removed her headset, exhaled, and laid back on her chair.

Cedric asks, 'Are you OK?'.

—' Yeah, it's just so fucking frustrating!' She replied.

She stayed like that for a minute, got up, went to the toilet, and came back after 5 minutes. It's unclear to me whether she went to pee or to cry even more. I have a gut feeling; I'd say she probably cried.

I get a handful of angry customers on the phone as well. They're angry because they have a problem with a product they bought, and they want an immediate resolution. That part is understandable. They get frustrated when they realise they're talking to an inexperienced agent who does not have a clue about what's going on. This is understandable, too. And to make matters worse, they lash out at me because of my lack of understanding and knowledge of the product that I represent. I feel horrible when that happens because I would be frustrated, too, if I was that customer. We should have more experienced agents taking the phone calls, and the newer agents should focus on emails to learn the ropes, especially after such shaky training. I don't have that luxury, so I tell customers I will call them back once I figure out what's what. It's easier with some than others, but I have no choice; I can't stay on the phone and sound stupid for several hours.

I receive an email one day. It has a video attached to it. It's from a man who set up two Bluetooth speakers and paired them so they can play simultaneously. The man says there's a 0.01-second delay between the two speakers, which bothers him. He has a very attentive ear, and he wonders if I can also hear the delay. I cannot. I trust that he knows what he's talking about, and he's so polite that I know he's not here to make a fuss; he really wants his problem fixed. I send him the usual troubleshooting steps. None of them are enough to fix the latency issue. He told me I could try to set up the same devices on my end and listen to 'Billie Jean' by Michael Jackson. He insists that I should listen to this song and not another. At this point, I don't know what to do. The pairing of two Bluetooth devices has only been mentioned in a PDF document I pretended to read a month ago. All the colleagues in the office are clueless, and I run out of options. I don't know what to do or say. Rose comes in that morning and tells us that the following week, two representatives of the speaker's brand will be in the office with us. They'll be here to ensure we provide support up to their standard and will help us in some cases if needed. This couldn't be better. The timing is perfect. I told my customer that experts would visit the office to review his case. I know it's a lie, but I'm sure it'll make him feel special. And most importantly, he'll leave me alone for the time being.

The following week, the two experts finally came in. We had a small talk before I mentioned my case with the Bluetooth delay to one of them. He reads the customer's email, squinting his eyes. He says it's funny, and he calls his partner so he can have a look. They both seem lost and confused, but they pretend they're not. They proceed to explain how Bluetooth works and how to pair two devices together. Though I'm sure this is an impressive anecdote to share at a dinner party, this is not at all what I asked for or what I need. They have yet to answer my question, and when I try to ask for specific details that could help my case, they stall and repeat themselves. They have no clue how to fix a latency issue. I told them that they were really helpful and thanked them for their non-assistance before erasing the fake smile off my face and scratching my head, wondering what to do with this customer now. I write the most confusing email I can put together and send it, hoping the customer will be knocked out by the lack of logic in my answer.

A new day begins. I arrive at the office, and I'm struck with a thought. I haven't seen Ron since he introduced himself on the first day. There was one time when he did buy us some doughnuts and left them on the desks for us, but that was it. That guy is nowhere to be found. I'm sure not running into my manager every day is normal, but the office isn't that big. Where is he hiding every day? He is washing everyone's mugs on the other side of the room, where I can't see him? I felt like I needed a manager to guide me through this, but it apparently isn't one of his tasks, ironically enough. And this isn't Rose's job either. They both have no hands in the actual job whatsoever, which makes me ask myself, 'Why are you guys even here?'. I know now that managers usually report numbers to their managers, who report them to their own managers, and so on. It's almost as if the higher-ups put as many barricades as they could between themselves and the bottom of the employee pyramid to make sure they never interact with us. The reported numbers include the number of phone calls we took, the number of emails we replied to, how long it took us to complete a case and how satisfied the customers are with us. Rose is the one who is reviewing these numbers. In my case, none of these metrics are good. I suddenly realise I'm not good at this. I don't solve half of the problems customers are bringing to me, and I'm not even doing a decent job pretending to care. I've not been prepared enough for this, and it's obvious to everyone at this point. The number of unsolved cases I have to my name is piling up, and the anxiety that comes with them builds up as well. I want to do well, but I don't know how. Rose only tells me that I'm not doing a good enough job, but she doesn't give me advice on how I can improve. The few people I can count on to help me with my cases aren't even that knowledgeable about the product. The so-called experts who came into the office a few days ago weren't either. Who has the answers to all of my questions, then?

This illustrates well what corporations are made of. They're half composed of people who already made their mark, are not afraid to be let go and spend their day pretending like they're the experts they're not. The other half is made of people like me, clueless and lost, who care to do a good job but have zero tools to achieve that. Alas, there are no more knowledgeable colleagues who know what they're talking about. I've seen many people faking it, but only on rare occasions would I find someone who has actual knowledge of the product. Knowledge that's not limited to what's on our training PDF. But these people are an extinct species since corporations care more about hiring complacent people who will abide by their stupid rules and illogical policy changes, people who will devote their heart and soul to the company because of the comfortable corporate position it offers. They believe PowerPoints and Q&A sections can replace the mind of a skilled professional, and they're convinced that such documentation is enough for new hires to become skilled themselves. Because the decision-makers surround themselves with sycophants, they never have to lose a day of sleep over their terrible judgment. No one would call them out for it; if someone does, it'll be at the bottom of the ladder. Only distorted echoes can be heard from the highest positions, which is not enough to disrupt and certainly not enough to challenge.

This is, overall, not the vision I had for my career. Purple isn't going to kick-start my career the way I thought it would. I took a moment to reflect and realised I hadn't grown roots here. I didn't bond with any of my colleagues, and I'm just as lost as I was on the first day. I decided to leave the company because it's not working for any of the parties here. I applied for a video-game-related job and ended up with a speaker's brand. I gather the courage and walk up to my manager's office. I let Rose know that I'm leaving. She's flagger-basted. It's a slap to her face. She does not bother to ask why I want to quit, and she tells me that HR will be in touch with me. I wait on the office couch, and one girl from HR comes out of the elevator with a big smile and a notebook. She comes to sit next to me, introduces herself and asks for the reason for my departure. I told her this was not what I envisioned the job to be. She nods and smiles. She gets up and tells me that she'll prepare the paper for the end of my contract. She didn't write a single thing on that notebook she carried. She goes back to the elevator and continues smiling as the door closes. Rose acted like I announced someone's death, and that girl acted like I announced I was getting a tattoo. I don't think either one of these reactions is appropriate, but I'm not concerned with this anymore; it's time for me to leave this company and find a better one. I need a lot more training, and thanks to this experience, I believe I can become a much better agent and start the corporate path I've already dreamed of.

Though my time with Purple was not what I hoped for, I learned about the job.

First, there are the agents. Agents pick up the call, answer emails, and chat with customers. They're the first line of contact between customers and the company.

To manage them, we have, of course, the managers. Managers can be former agents who got promoted to a higher role, or external employees who were brought in for their organisation skills. Managers do not have any involvement in customer contacts most of the time. Their job is to make sure that agents hit their targets every week, and act in consequence if they don't. They report directly to their own manager, who reports to their manager, and so on.

Quality agents are people who supervise the contact with customers to make sure they meet the requirements they set. They listen to calls, read the email chain between an agent and a customer, and rate the interaction based on a grid they created. This will determine if the agent did their job correctly or not. Some of the criteria of this grid include the introduction of the call, whether the agent was professional, and whether the customer's problem was solved. This notation system is entirely situational since sometimes problems can't be solved. Complying with quality standards can be challenging, especially when their guidelines often change and are designed to be unreachable.

The main company is the owner of the product, on which we, agents, will provide support. If a company makes shoes, agents will provide support about the shoes, refund orders, take care of exchanges, and track deliveries. The company has two choices: they can either have their own support department, which means they'll have to invest in equipment, employees, contracts and all the necessary stuff to create a functioning support. The other choice is to hire a third party, an outsource, so they can take care of the support for them.

The outsourcing company is hired by the main company and will handle contracting employees, providing them with the equipment they need, and training them on the product. Because the main company is paying for the outsourcing, they are quite exigent with the quality of service they want the agents to provide. This means they'll be attentive to all the numbers the outsourced reports will provide: a number of cases solved, customer satisfaction, amount of refunds given… The pressure is high for the outsource as they have to keep the main company happy to receive funding, or they'll be out of business. Some penalties also exist, such as if the main company isn't happy with some of the numbers being reported, they can reduce the check they're sending. Departments can also be entirely shut down if the main company decides that another outsource can do the job better or for less money. To make sure they remain on top of their game, the outsourcing company cracks the whip on their directors, so they can crack the whip on managers, all the way down until it reaches support agents on which the whip hits the hardest.

At last, the term tools refers to the different systems I use to deal with cases. Emails and phone calls are coming through a system and I have a variety of tools I can use to solve issues. There is one payment tool where I can initiate refunds, another tool to manage accounts, etc.

Knowing this is going to be valuable going forward.

Chapter 3: Blue

I'm still attached to the idea of a corporate career, but I want to do things differently this time. I need to work for a company I know and for a product I understand, with better preparation overall. After my failed attempt at climbing the corporate ladder in Amsterdam, I came back to Italy. I started searching for new opportunities. I sent my resume and uploaded it to a website, and I imagine it was sent to recruiters. Within the first week, I receive three job offers, all interesting to me. It's worth noting that none of these jobs has the title' Customer Support' in their job offer titles. It is always something different. 'Experience Provider' or 'Confirmed Advisor'. Almost as if the term 'Customer Service' was Lord Voldemort's name, and no one dared to speak it.

The first offer I received was for a major streaming platform. The salary they offer is quite low, despite working for a big company. The second one is for one of the biggest airlines in Europe. Once again, the salary they offer is low. Realistically, the salary isn't that low. Compared to other wages in the same country, it's actually above average and makes living comfortably easy. *It just seemed low to me.* And although the recruiters swore that it was enough to make a living, I wouldn't buy it. The jobs they offered were in major cities. Every city centre in Europe has the same problem:

there are way too many people and not enough accommodation. This makes the cost of living higher than it should be and consequently doubles the price I would normally pay for renting. I say double, and I'm being nice here. After doing some math, I figured that wherever I would go, half of my salary would go towards rent. It was all about making the other half as big as it could be. And there came the last and final offer. It arrived a Thursday morning, freshly delivered via email, a job in Dublin for a big company which specialized in bookings, rentals, hotels, these kinds of things. Unlike my job in Purple, this position is a work-from-home position. I still have to be in Ireland, but I don't have to be in an office; I can stay in my bedroom to work. It seemed too good to be true. Not only do I know this company (which is a change; the previous one I worked for, I just pretended to know), but it's also one of the leaders in this market. The customer service is handled by an outsourcing company, Blue. They're hired by the main company to provide support, and they will be hiring me as well. This is by far the best offer I received for the best product and company. The salary they offer is high. It was the highest I've ever been offered. On top of an already high salary, the company offered all sorts of bonuses based on performance. Hundreds of euros could be added to my salary if I were to perform well in my job. *This is so easy.* I'm already envisioning myself earning tens of bonuses, doubling my salary and drinking martinis on a yacht. Or a fisherman's boat, whatever they have in Ireland. If there is a catch behind the offer, I don't care to get caught. I dropped the two other recruiting processes to focus solely on this one. Like the previous ones, they sent me a few tests for me to pass. Mostly grammar, spelling, and elocution; they wanted to know if I could take a phone call or write an email in each language I was going to be speaking. The results came in after a few days only, and I was accepted. The recruiter, a nice lady, seems more excited than I am about the idea of me joining the company. *What a nice lady,* I thought. This is before I learn about recruiters' commissions. She sent a bunch of documents and contracts to sign, and I even got an offer so they would pay for my apartment for the first weeks. I finished all my paperwork and got in touch with the agency that will provide accommodation for me. They ask me to send some money for a non-refundable deposit. I'm a bit surprised that the recruiter did not mention it, but I have no choice but to pay since I already signed a bunch of contracts. I bring this up to the recruiter, and she says:

'Oh yeah, sorry for the bad surprise'.

This is a bit of a red flag but nonetheless, I get moving and the next thing I know I am in a plane taking off to join my new dream job in Dublin.

I probably should've done my research more properly. The only thing I knew about Ireland was what I was sent in an email. I received a 10-page PDF with pictures of Dublin, all saturated to make it bright and colourful. The city is actually like this, one week per year when there's actually sunshine. The rest of the time, it's mostly grey and raining. But hey, who's gonna complain about the weather when I'm getting paid this much? A taxi driver comes to pick me up at the airport and takes me to the temporary accommodation my company so kindly provided. Another thing quickly started to worry me: the infrastructure of the building I was dropped at. The taxi driver asked for my autograph so he could give the invoice to the company. He gave me my suitcase and left me in front of this narrow door, between a pub and a Christian relics store. On the wall, there's a big poster for a hair salon, which I have no idea where to find. It certainly isn't in this street. As I enter, I climb the stairs. They're tiny. My room is on the 2nd floor. It's a nice room. A double bed, a nice window, natural light. I can't complain. It's quite spacious as well; I have a desk, a closet, and a mirror. It becomes interesting when I explore the rest of the house. I quickly find out that I'm sharing this house with seven other people. This also was not mentioned by that honest recruiter. We have one tiny kitchen and two bathrooms, one of which is apparently only for the senior members of this house sharing. Some of them live here permanently and have been for quite some time. Though I can't say that this house is dirty, it certainly isn't living up to the expectations I had in my head. I genuinely thought that a big company like this one would pay for a private apartment with modern furniture on the last floor of a brand-new building with a doorman. This was the image I envisioned before taking off, the one I described to my friends and family. And now here I am, sharing my house with students, divorced dads and early-retired seamstresses. What the fuck is that. I thought I made it big when I signed a contract offering so much money. It is simply the first wake-up call: I'm not anyone important, this job is not highly ranked, and this is what I got myself into. This company did everything it could to conceal the reality of life here. It's the equivalent of moments in cartoons when they have a cutout falling, revealing something a lot worse behind. I tried to reassure myself. Not much time to think, though, as I receive a phone call:

'Your working equipment is here', informs the delivery guy over the phone.

I opened the door to that same guy, and he dropped the box in front of me.

'Bye'.

Is … that it? Are you really leaving this expensive brand-new MacBook with my name engraved on it like that? No signatures required? The box is the size of my suitcase. It is heavy, not properly taped, and a lot of papers are glued to it; some are old and thorned, and some seem more recent. These have my name on it. Are they reusing the box? *Perhaps an eco-friendly company.* I open the box and get another slap in the face as to what I'm embarking on. The equipment is not new. It's actually been used quite a lot if I judge by the smell, the touch and all the tangled wires at the bottom of the box.

It's not a great setup, either. The screen is a few years old. Nothing has been cleaned; there's some hardened sweat on the mouse and crisps leftovers on the keyboard. All my dreams of a brand-new laptop vanish as I disinfect all of this.

I venture into the kitchen and find only 2 pans and an impressive collection of mugs which will be used as glasses. There is one tiny fridge which we will all share (there are 8 of us, as a friendly reminder) and still the fridge was empty. No one has anything for themselves here. There are a few sodas, some butter, and that is it. What are they all eating? Are they eating outside every day? Or not eating at all? I know that I left Italy, but I didn't mean for Italy to leave me. How am I going to cook in this horrible kitchen? There's not even a drain for the pasta. There's no garlic press. And with the humidity that I feel in the air, I don't think my basil would survive 3 days without starting to rot. Eating my dishes every day is vital for me. This feels like a prison. I'm outraged by the lack of life in the kitchen. With eight people under the same roof, it's a crime that all of us have to resort to instant noodles for dinner.

I met my housemates, and one of them was particularly happy to see me. He's Spanish, a student, and the same age as me. I asked him about the kitchen situation, and he told me that most of the housemates eat takeaway food in their bedrooms. I feel shivers all over my body. He shows me his room, and I'm not sure whether I should cry or laugh. I thought Harry Potter had it hard beneath the staircase, but this was something else. He is living on the last floor of this narrow building, in what was previously, for sure, the attic. There are no windows, only a bed big enough for half a Spanish like him and a tiny desk on which I'm not sure a computer could fit. At this moment, I wonder if there was ever a possibility for me to be in a similar room. Did I get the bigger room because my company pays for it and wants to make sure I can live and work comfortably? Or did I just win the lottery with this twisted rental company that's overcharging these poor people to live in terrible conditions? I offered to hang out in my room to make sure there was enough oxygen for the two of us, but after an hour, we decided it was best to get out of the house. I explored the city for a little bit before coming back home. I'm starting to work the following day, and I want to be in the best shape possible.

My training starts on the next day. It is 8 a.m. I plugged my computer in and joined the meeting I was invited to. It's a bit weird; no one talks. No one has their webcam turned on. Then, the trainer, Ron, comes in and starts breaking the ice. It's not an easy task to get 20 strangers to talk to each other and build relationships through a screen. He does a terrific job, though. He's funny and engaging, and he never lets any moment of silence last for too long. He's the man for the job. And he looks like he's enjoying it. My faith in the company is coming back. Finally, something good is happening. The first employee I'm in contact with is nice, charismatic and super helpful. If everyone has that same mentality, I'll fit right in. He has the task of training us to make us ready to go live at the end of the month. By the end of the month, we'll have to know enough about the company, the procedures, the system we're using, and how to reply to all types of queries.

A month sounds like a lot of time to get the preparation needed to handle calls, but the time runs out quickly when we lose days trying to set up some of the guys' equipment. Some of us follow the training on other people's computers that we live with because our own can't work or burned. I didn't believe it either before they mentioned the smoke coming out of the computer. The first day is supposed to be an introduction call. Instead, it is a 3-hour-long call between Ron and another recruit, a 40-year-old Italian woman who can't get her screen to work. After some intense troubleshooting, it was determined that the screen was not plugged in and thus couldn't work. We lost 3 hours of training for that. The next day, another colleague can't get their login credentials to work. And the next day, another one. To be honest, we don't do much during the first week.

The weeks go by, and I slowly learn about the product. Ron shows us the website, how to make a booking, select dates, etc. We're being shown what the customer interface looks like, which is nice. We don't see much of our own interface as agents, though. We get a briefing on what's expected of us and how to answer customers when they call. For the rest, Ron says we'll have relevant resources available to help us, and we can always message him if needed. From mornings to evenings, we read these resources and have quizzes at the end of them to make sure we understand them. I once again feel like a monkey in a laboratory, with a round-shaped cylinder to put in a round-shaped hole. I read about the company and how it was founded. The success story of the CEOs and how they revolutionize the world once again. I'd like to know about my daily tasks and how to take care of them, but this seems more important to Blue. Three weeks of training go by, and we meet with Ron at the end of each day. He asks if we have any questions, but we never ask any because we just want to be done with our day.

During this training, I get to meet new people and see new faces on my computer screen every day. Some of them are Italian like me, so I naturally connect faster with them than with the rest of the guys. I didn't come here to create my own mafia abroad, though, so I make sure to reach out to as many of my colleagues as I can. I will be spending the next few weeks with them, and some of them might even end up in my team after we're done with the training. We exchange numbers and create a group chat so we can communicate outside of working platforms, which is easier but also for more freedom of speech. There isn't a lot to complain about, however. We just started, so the only things we discussed were the funny anecdotes we had experienced together.

'Do you guys remember when I couldn't turn on my computer for 3 hours?' the Italian woman says.

We send laughing emojis. We're still shy, I guess. We get more and more comfortable with each other as time passes and start to chat more regularly. I'm not living with anyone who works for Blue, though some of my colleagues ended up together in their temporary accommodations. There are even discussions about sharing houses. As training is coming to an end in a week, we decide to meet up on the weekend. We set up a time and date, to meet at a pub.

The pubs are the heart of Ireland. It's a strange concept to me, but I'm open to new ideas. I'm quite curious as well. I always heard that wild things happen in pubs, and I'm eager to know which ones. I arrive at 7 p.m. at the pub where I'm supposed to meet my colleagues. Some of them are already here. We look at each other, confirming our names and kissing awkwardly. The Spaniards are hugging. The Frenchies are kissing on the cheeks. Practice makes perfect; I'll know what to do with each nationality next time. We go inside and order pints of beer. I've never been a fan of beer, personally. I find the taste to be similar to piss. There aren't many options outside beers, though, so I'm compelled to order a pint. The glass is larger than any I've ever been served before. It's also a lot more expensive than anything I can order in Italy. This is going to last for the night, and I'm not even sure that I will be finishing it. I walk up to my table and find a seat. My group is already having conversations. Those who speak the same languages tend to stay together, but in an effort to mix, we all make efforts to keep our discussions in English. I learn about my colleagues. Some of them just dropped out of college; others lost their jobs before applying for this one. I'm surprised that no one applied for this job willingly. It sounds like it was everyone's plan B. I'm the youngest member of the group, and when I tell everyone that I just finished high school, they don't believe it. I get it; it's weird that there's such an age gap between some of us, but I don't mind. We all have one thing in common, though: we are sure that there isn't any future in our own countries. We're all disappointed by politics and discouraged by the economy. We don't talk about work all that much. We make quick references to previous situations, like the computer fuming, but that's it. We all seem to be enjoying ourselves for now. One Italian guy says he has friends who are working for Blue. He says they hate it and want to quit. We laugh at him. Why would they want to quit such a cool job? I mean, look at us, we're all in a pub in Dublin because of Blue. Regardless of what the job is or isn't, this is an experience I never would've been able to have if it weren't for them. I just assume that his friends are Italian and grumpy like we all are and decide to shake it off. That comment won't ruin my night. We spent a few hours talking at a surface level just to break the ice. I'm starting to put names on faces. I already know these faces in a way. I discover who's tall and who's not. I'm seeing the sides of people's visages, as opposed to only having them face me on video conferences. I'm pretty content with my night. I turned colleagues into friends, and I can now say that my contact list has expanded beyond borders. I have friends from different countries, and I find it extraordinary. I do note that none of my colleagues are Irish, though. Now that I think about it, the only Irish I met are the managers. There aren't any Irish agents. I suppose that makes sense because they would need to speak a second language to be an agent. The fact remains that they seem to be having higher positions in the company and aren't really hanging out with us all that much. After a while, I decided to go home to rest. I leave half of my pint on the table. I can't finish it.

On the last day of training and we have to pass a test to know if we can start working for Blue or not. We were told this from the beginning of the training that there would be a test to make sure we did follow what was taught. We're given 2 hours and a series of questions. At the end of the day, the trainer meets with us to announce the results.

The trainer is not happy. He accuses us of cheating. And he is right. We have a WhatsApp group on which we are sending each other the answers to the test. He did notice it because the question 27, which was a basic and simple question, was not correctly answered by anyone. We all had the same answer and it was obvious that anyone who's been listening to the training we had couldn't get it wrong.

'If it sounds like a duck, walks like a duck…' he says.

Some people in the group chat are panicking. They're asking if we should tell him the truth. Maybe he'll be more forgiving if we confess? I tell them we shouldn't. When in doubt, denying is always easier. Ron tells us that this is grounds for disqualification and that we won't be passing the final test. This scares most of my colleagues. They all left their countries to be here. If they can't get the job, it would be terrible. But I know an empty threat when I see one. This company flew us here so we could do the job no one else wanted to do; they weren't going to let go of us that easily. We all got out of the situation unharmed, though, since it was determined that the form we used for the test did not register our answers correctly. The moment the trainer notices, he apologizes and says he'll never doubt us again. This is a valuable lesson. When caught, my loyalty to my colleagues is what will get me out of trouble. Covering each other's back is key to surviving in the corporate world, and this is the first taste we had of a true bonding experience against the oppressor.

Passing this test also means that the training comes to an end, and that the following week will be my first week as an agent going live. I'm nervous. I'm going to take calls. This is my first time working from home. There's no one around me now to help if I'm lost. I spend the rest of the weekend moving into my new house since my time in this temporary accommodation is coming to an end.

Here it is. My first day as an agent taking calls. I turn on my computer, login and start searching for my first email to reply to. After 3 minutes, I hear a buzzing sound in my ear and then a white noise. For a few seconds, I can't hear anything and then it comes.

'Hello?' someone is talking to me.

—'Hello?' I ask, just as confused as they sound.

—'Ah! There you are! They told me the call was being transferred.'

It was a customer. They called the support number and got me on the phone without me knowing. The phone barely rang for me and automatically picked up. I did not have an option to refuse or avoid the call. That sounds benign, but it feels so violent. I cannot avoid the calls. I know I signed up for calls, but it is one thing to pick up the phone and introduce myself, and it's another to have the phone thrown at me like a task I need to accomplish immediately. I can be a food tester, but that does not mean someone is going to shove food down my throat. But here it is the case. They're shoving the calls down my throat. Thankfully, that first customer is really nice. She's a young woman asking for basic information about refunds, which I'm not able to answer right away because I'm second-guessing myself on the first day. I told her that I would call her back once I found out the answer to her question, even though I had no idea how to initiate a callback or where to find that answer. But I will eventually call her back later that day. When people call the customer support of a company, they might get an experienced agent who's been working here for 2 years or a brand-new recruit who's just finished their training. They would probably prefer to get the more experienced agent on the line, but I can assure them that no one wants that more than us new recruits. After the call ended, I was a bit taken aback. I am now aware that calls can come at any moment, and this is not the easy, peaceful job I thought it would be. For 8 hours, I will be at the mercy of anyone calling, and I won't have any other choice but to engage immediately after the first buzzing sound. This was not mentioned at all in the training or the recruitment process. I assume they had to come up with this automated pick-up process because past agents might've figured out how to get out of the phone queue, but I'm still shocked that this is what it has come down to for us.

The job took an unexpected turn in a matter of minutes during my first day. It changes my perspective on what this was going to be once again, and this time I am sure that no more good news was to come, only deceit.

Later that first day, I'm invited to a team meeting. When I joined, I saw most of my colleagues who were trained with me and my manager, Robert. This is the first I'm meeting with him. He seems really nice; he's in his 30s and has a really calm tone. He tries to make us comfortable and tells us that we can count on him for anything we need. Those who try to ask him for help aren't being assisted, though. He seems to know less than us about the job and never has an answer to anything. This does not bother me. All I want is someone nice who's not going to make my life hard. And that's exactly who he is.

I wake up 30 minutes before my shift starts. I turn on my computer and make sure to update my working status to 'Available' at 8:00 a.m. sharp. I was told that I couldn't be late, so 8 sharp it is. A new day begins, and a new phone call picks up automatically. Usually, 5 minutes after I start my shift, the phone rings. Someone is always trying to call Blue's support. Funnily enough, the most pressing issues never occur in the morning. It's always a dumb question or a refund request that could've waited for another week. I wonder if these people miss me when they can't reach out to me outside of business hours. Did they set an alarm to make sure to be the first one to call today? I'm instantly thrown into the lion pit and have to be ready to face anything. I do everything I'm told; I greet the user accordingly, create a case for our own documentation and classify it with care. I also make sure to verify the account ownership by asking the user a variety of personal questions. After the call ends, I send an email to summarize what we talked about. It's a lot of documentation and a lot of notes to take. The tiniest details have to be put in writing: these are the guidelines I have to follow. When I don't have a call, I have to work on emails. The phone can ring again at any moment, interrupting me in the middle of another email case. Now I understand why they asked me if I could do multiple tasks. This is great for my attention deficit, and it is even better to mix things up when talking to one user about another one's case. But productivity is key, and this is how we roll here. The days pass, and just like in my previous job, a routine starts. I take calls for 8 hours a day, and I don't see how time flies. I feel it in the moment but not afterwards. I learn a lot about the product and I'm not as clueless as I was before. I know what to answer in most cases, and if I don't, I feel comfortable telling the user that I will call them back once I figure it out. Blue heavily encourages this, mostly because it boosts the number of outbound calls we make. They can show that number to the main company to make them happy. The list of issues I have to take care of varies from refunds to help with listing settings, booking modification, cancellation, and account settings. The people I talk to are also quite diverse; some are adults and don't have time to talk on the phone because of their work. Some are retired and have all the time in the world. Younger people prefer to talk via email and usually don't answer when I call them. Sometimes, I get called by the police for investigations, sometimes by a celebrity's agent to book them a room somewhere. I also get influencers on the phone who want a free booking because they're famous on Instagram. The list is endless, and no call resembles the previous one. Most of these exchanges are nice. People are usually more polite on the phone, but when they are rude, they really lash out at me. It's the case when they're asking for a refund that I can't give. I have a speech, an explanation, and an empathy statement. It does not matter. When a person is losing money, it makes them see red. And I get that. My job is to be on the receiving end and apologize until they hang up and accept their loss. It can take a while. Sometimes, they ask to speak to a manager, or they threaten to sue the company. We don't really do anything differently, though, since managers couldn't care less to talk with them, and legal threats are not promises. The call ends, and the day continues. Once a case is closed, it counts as a resolution for me, regardless of whether I fixed a problem or not. Denying a refund and closing a case counts as a resolution. I can see how many cases I solve per week on my system. Each week, that number resets. By the end of the week, I have to have a minimum of resolutions, so it is considered a good performance. During my first weeks, my managers cut me some slack as I didn't have to reach a high number. As time goes by, that target slowly increases until I'm expected to perform a lot more. Alongside these targets, I'm given a bunch of other metrics I need to respect. I have a satisfaction score, a handling time for my case, contact duration, and so on. Combined with the extremely precise documentation of my work, I become quickly overwhelmed with how many factors I have to take into account and respect each week. There's no real forgiveness for error since a single mistake can cost me a lot. The numbers are reviewed by my manager, and the documentation of my case is reviewed by a team called Quality. They're the company's inspectors, and they check the tiniest comp in the shortest sentence. I like to imagine them with a magnifying glass, reading my messages. They also listen to my calls since they're recorded. They review the tone I have with the customer when I engage with them, if I'm helpful and professional, that sort of thing. They also review the notes I took during my calls, which I take while I'm on a call, so it's never a well-written poem. They go easy on me at first, but they also make it clear that I have to step up my game every week. This creates the foundations of a stressful working environment, which will only become tougher as time passes.

I've been working for Blue for a while now, so this was meant to happen. The phone rings once again. I greet the person on the phone, and they immediately cut me off to shout at me. I'm speechless. I knew this was coming, and this is it. They're yelling and demanding an immediate refund for a booking they can no longer attend. Unfortunately for them (and for me), they're not eligible for a refund, and I have to break the news for them. I tell them a few times, but the situation quickly escalates. They start shouting and insulting me with a list of names that becomes longer by the second. They're coming up with them so rapidly that Eminem would be proud. I'm terrified on the other side of the line. I don't know how to react. I'm not sure if I should raise my voice as well. I'm probably going to get in trouble if I do. Should I cry? Should I quit? Should I start singing a song? I ask myself all kinds of questions while the user on the phone gets even more irritated that I don't answer.

The longer I wait, the worse it gets. I have to act now before the bomb explodes. I scan my room around, searching for something that can help. I saw it, and I decided to go for it. I unplug my Wi-Fi router. This cuts my Internet connection and instantly puts an end to my misery. The phone icon becomes a loading circle. I start taking notes while the Wi-Fi resets. I mentioned that my Wi-Fi dropped during the call, and I will be sending the user an email instead. After a minute, the Wi-Fi started to work again, and I reconnected with the user. I'm mortified. The call never ended.

'Hello?? ARE YOU STILL THERE???' they're shouting.

I don't move. I stop breathing. I don't want them to hear me make a sound. I went for the Internet solution, and I'm sticking to it. I hang up the call manually by clicking on the red phone icon, which I'm never supposed to do. Since I'm still fairly new, I'm hoping that I can get away with it. Also, there has been enough silence in the call for my explanation to be credible if anyone ever cares to listen to the call to check. I'm shocked to learn that Blue's phone system is Internet-proof. Nothing can keep me away from these users shouting at me. Nothing can keep me safe. I'm at the mercy of ruthless people in the comfort of my own home. What will I do with the next one? Am I just supposed to endure this endlessly? The phone rings. I have 2 seconds to start talking again. My heart is in my throat. I barely make a sound when I hear a woman's voice. This is not the same user. I'm relieved. I feel so much lighter. This woman is nice, and I try to stay on the line with her for as long as I can. That way, the previous guy can't get me on the phone again because I'm already busy with someone else. This means that a colleague of mine is facing the wrath of that idiot who surely called again. I feel bad that I let that guy on the loose. I have no time to think about it, though: I have a new case to take care of and lines of documentation to write. The clock is ticking, and so is my timer. I'll worry about this when I have time.

Because the job started at such a fast pace, we were told that some people were there to help us get through the day. They're called 'Angels', though I would have called them demons, but that's beside the point. Angels are here to assist us with our cases. We can contact them if we're stuck on a case, and they're supposed to help us find the answer to our problem. In all fairness, most of them are friendly and helpful. I will be the first to admit that I often rush to their assistance before doing anything else, even though I am supposed to do some research on my end and contact them only if I find nothing. As time passes, I reach out less and less to them and only use this joker card in times of desperate need. To get assistance from an angel, I have to fill out a form and send it to an automated system. The form asks for details of the case, links to articles I already went through to search for an answer and my case number. One available agent will pick up my form and come back to me via a direct message to help me. This is fast enough when I'm on emails, but it feels like an eternity on a call. We have a rule stating that we can put a customer on hold as much as we want to find the answer to their query. The rule also states that we should return to the user every few minutes to let them know we're still working on their case. Filling out the form and waiting until an angel comes back to me usually takes 5–10 minutes. Each 2–3 minutes, I tell the customer that I'm making some progress and close to finding an answer. It gets old quickly, and a customer can only be said to wait for so long. I need help now.

On that day, I encountered that situation. After a few back-and-forths while keeping my customer waiting on the phone, an angel messaged me. She said she was reviewing my case and would provide me with an answer in a few minutes. I waited patiently, watching the three little dots in our conversation windows wiggle until she was done typing her message.

'Did you read this article?'. She sends me a link to a help article on our website.

'Yes, I did! :-), I didn't find the answer in it :-(' I reply.

I already mentioned that article in the form I had to fill out to contact her. She knows I read it. Why is she asking me if I did? Maybe I missed something, but in this case, it would be more helpful to point out the part that I missed rather than insinuate that I'm a lazy larva.

'The answer is in the article'. She closes the chat.

This specific angel was not helpful at all. She preferred to let me handle a case by myself, knowing that I already put a customer on hold for 15 minutes and that I didn't have an answer for them. Like in other jobs, I get accustomed to my colleagues and know which ones are nice and which ones I don't want to talk to. Some angels are lovely, whereas others are purely diabolical. It's strange to me that a position which requires patience, empathy and altruism would be given to corporate sadists. When I have the misfortune of getting picked by an evil angel, I know my case will not be solved, and I cannot count on them to get help. I understand they're here to help us and not do the job for us. Having said that, I integrated the fact that I need to investigate before contacting them. Now, most help articles are outdated and confusing. The internal search system we have has been coded by an illiterate ostrich. When I type in 'window', I get results for 'pizzas'. None of the articles I need to come up in the search results when I search for them. When I find one, it's pages long and too generic to apply to most situations. Each case is different, and customers have their own specificities, meaning that general statements cannot reflect and bring a solution to every scenario. That is why I need the support of an angel from time to time. And some angels do a great job backing us up. Others will receive my call for help while letting me burn down with a fire extinguisher in their hand.

I am bitter about this. Let's say that I actually did not do any research on my end before contacting an angel (which I totally didn't sometimes, out of laziness). Isn't it their job to help us anyway? When I did my interview for this job, I pretended that helping others was my passion. And that's what I have to do now. How can they get away with being un-assisting passive-aggressive avatars?

One of my colleagues messages the training group chat. He wants us to all meet again to discuss how the job is going and what has changed for us since we're no longer on the same team. Most of the group accepted, but only a few declined the invitation or did not reply. We have decided to meet at a pub over the weekend. I will be late because I am working that Saturday, and I'm not the only one. When I arrive, I'm happy to see these familiar faces again. The vibe is a bit different. We make small talk, but we quickly circle back to work-related conversations. I just arrived, and I'm being told what I missed. Mostly gossip about managers. I excuse myself to go to order a pint. I challenge myself to finish it tonight. After all, I worked hard this week, and I have been working the whole day, too. I return to the table and catch them continuing their discussion about managers. They're in a different team, so I don't know who their manager is, but they don't seem to mind. They continue. As if I knew who they were referring to. I catch minor complaints about the job and feel they're slightly disappointed. Now that we started seeing what our tasks look like, we're all disenchanted. I only have a little professional experience, and I'm grateful to be here, so I don't really want to jump on that train. I still recognise that what they're saying is valid, and I agree with most of it. I find some of them to be exaggerating, though. I sit there and listen to various arguments about our schedule, our equipment, the management... The hours pass, and I don't realise that I work overtime, listening to complaints all over again. I look down at my pint; it's nearly finished. I don't have the strength to order another one or listen to them more. I finish my glass, bottoms up, and I go home. This is a weird night. I still feel happy about the job, but some parts of me are warning me about how fast reality is catching up with me. I'm no longer sure this is going to be the pleasant walk in the park I thought it was going to be. Is it the same for all customer support jobs? Or do I need to choose my companies better? I'm confused. I fall asleep and set my alarm for the next day. I'm going to be working on Sunday, too.

We get news one night that a global pandemic of Covid is upon us, and a lockdown is about to begin. Just as we thought we were starting a new life, we're being hit with staying home for a few months. This has not changed much for me personally since I work from home. However, this has changed my work a lot.

The next day hits me like a wave. All the phone lines are already saturated at 8 a.m. People from all over the world are calling to ask if we will refund them since we're going on lockdown, and they can't travel anymore. I know what is expected of me. I have to tell them no. There are policies that they accepted when they made their booking and policies that clearly state whether they can get a refund or not. And although that policy does not mention anything about a wave of COVID-19, our instructions are clear: we are not refunding anyone.

I think this is unfair. And I'm not the only one in my team who thinks so. I'm seeing the amounts these people spent on their bookings. It sounds insane that a father who spent $2,000 in a hotel for next year's family vacations can't be refunded now. If I pay for a service which can't be provided, I would expect to be refunded, regardless of the reasons. I want to do something for these people, but my system permissions do not allow me to issue a refund on my own. I come up with a plan. I know that if the cancellation is made by us, these people will be refunded. This is my secret weapon. If anyone yells at me and does not take no for an answer, I will transfer the case to my colleagues from a higher department and ask them to perform the cancellation. I know that from the moment I inform the user about this cancellation process, they have to do it. The golden rule in customer service is that if an agent promises something, even if it is against the company's policies, users are entitled to ask for it. If they've been promised something, they will get it. This can be used in a variety of contexts. For example, if a booking is cancelled at the last minute for any reason and an agent on the phone says the company will pay for a hotel, the company will pay for a hotel. For any hotel. If there were no previous mentions of a particular hotel or a price range they must stick to, then bingo. They can book a night in the Hilton Hotel at the company's expense. When the time comes to send the bill, they can refer the agent to the recorded call they made when this offer was made.

I quickly got discovered, and my manager asked me to stop doing this immediately. I pretend like I didn't know I shouldn't have done this. No more refunds for the folks calling in. I don't know who I feel sorrier for. Them, for not getting their money back, or me having to deal with the aftermath?

The terms in which a booking was made determine whether users can get a refund or not if they were to cancel. For example, a hotel that knows they can get a booking anytime will be more likely to let people cancel for free, meaning that they will get back all the money they spent on the booking. On the other hand, if a private party rents their apartment and relies heavily on the money to make a living, they tend to have stricter policies and generally do not refund guests if they cancel their booking. They're not getting a refund if they booked a reservation with the no-refund policy. This seems pretty straightforward, but most customers have a hard time taking no for an answer. I understand because, as a customer, I would want to get a refund in the event of a cancellation. However, the terms and conditions that they accept without reading most of the time make them ineligible to claim any refund whatsoever. There are a few rare exceptions in which they can get a refund despite having booked with the no-refund policy. This includes having a relative who died or being the victim of a natural catastrophe. It also included 'global pandemics' before the Covid outburst. They quickly changed their terms to include global pandemics minus the COVID-19 one. Funnily enough, I did get to contact Blue's support once a year before applying for them. I had booked a villa in Spain in which I was supposed to spend two weeks with my at-the-time boyfriend. The terms were clear: We wouldn't get a refund if we were to cancel. During an unfortunate event, he got robbed in Colombia and consequently got stolen his wallet and passport, making him unable to leave the country to join me in Spain. I was tasked to call Blue's support to ask if we could get a refund, even though we did not qualify for one per the terms of service. When I mentioned the story, I could tell the agent on the line did not know what to say. I would find myself in her position a year later, so I can understand how easy it is to be at a loss for words when someone drops a bomb like this on you. After awkward exchanges, she asked if I could send her proof. I thought about sending pictures of my boyfriend comically turning his pockets inside out to show they're empty while making a sad face. But I had to do this seriously to get our money back. After all, he had already been robbed once this week. By some miracle, we managed to send a picture of his old passport and a supermarket receipt, which I'm still unsure why this helped. But it worked. We did get the money back in full. I became an employee for the same company a year after that incident, and I never thought about checking the notes the agent left on my case that day. I really want to check them now. I want to know if she just typed 'lol' when mentioning the receipt we sent or if she accidentally clicked on the refund button and had to pretend she did it intentionally when replying to us. I will never know. Visiting people's accounts is a big no-no, despite being what we have to do every day. The general rule of thumb is that I should only visit the account of the customer contacting me. If I were to visit someone else's account, I would have to leave a note saying why I was there and leave my case number for documentation. If I had the misfortune of visiting someone's account without saying why, I would get in big trouble. This seems exaggerated, but the company takes it very seriously. This is heavily monitored, and I will get a strike for doing this. It is said that they put this measure in place to prevent people from accessing their own accounts to add money in the form of a travel credit and also to make sure no one would stalk Kylie Jenner by getting the address to her hotel. Yes, even she uses the platform.

The aggravating circumstances in which one could find themselves eligible for a refund change every once in a while. Another change I witnessed is the 'loss of a relative' policy. If someone has to cancel a booking last minute because their grandma sadly passed away and they have to attend the funeral, they will qualify for an exceptional refund. This is human and empathetic. But humanity gets easily thrown out of the window by its big sister, 'Profit', when this one feels threatened. It seems that grandmas were dropping like flies during COVID-19, and that excuse must've cost too much money for the company to keep in place. As a result, the terms were changed so that they would issue a refund if they lost direct parents but no longer grandparents. This also does not include cool aunts or close cousins. It has to be a mom. It's sad when the one good thing the company is doing correctly suddenly stops for the wrong reasons. I find this change to be vicious, too. The death of someone's parents is such a devastating loss that no one would even think about bookings and reservations. By the time it crosses their mind, it's likely that their reservation ended days ago, rendering them unable to claim anything back since they're past the reservation date. Perhaps Blue is counting on that to ensure no one uses this policy anymore except people who hate their parents, of course.

I work from home in an apartment I share with another Italian girl. She is working the same job as me, for the same company. She receives a call one day from a woman informing her that she has to cancel her booking because her mother has passed away. My housemate offered her sympathies and asked for the proper documentation to be sent, as it is required to verify the claim and document the case. That mother must've been an awful one because she had freshly died the same morning her daughter called. Consequently, no certificate of death has been issued yet. The madness of this job often leaves room for my imagination, and I love trying to picture what people look like when they call for support. I picture this woman in her living room next to her mom's corpse after tragically succumbing to a heart attack. She called the support as she was struggling to find the reservation number for her booking on the laptop. Once she hung up with us, I picture her calling the restaurant that just delivered her lunch, asking if she could get a refund for the second pizza she ordered and that no one ate in the end. Possibly after that, she calls an ambulance.

I'm going to great lengths to transform a traumatic event into a comical one so that I don't lose my mind in the process. I can't believe someone in their right mind would contact Blue's support, out of all people, on the same day their mother died. I tried to reason with myself: maybe this person deals with grief differently. I shouldn't judge customers without knowing the full story. Two days later, she came back via email:

'Good news! I finally got the death certificate:-)'.

I'm definitely judging her now, and I won't have any remorse. I'm slowly beginning to understand why customer support agents have that reputation for being cold and robotic. We're not prepared to react to such situations. A customer contacts us to joyfully deliver her mother's death certificate; what do we reply? '*Enjoy the funeral*'? We have to put some distance between us and these daily cases; some of them are too heavy to handle, and I never know when the next one is about to hit. A lot of my colleagues are mentally exhausted. I wonder how agents who've been working here for years can still be doing the same thing after all this time.

Thankfully, some interactions are a lot lighter. Sometimes, the host just wants to know how many toilet paper rolls they're obliged to provide each day to their guest. One guest was apparently too prolific on the toilet, and for economic reasons, the host wouldn't give them new rolls unless they knew they were obliged by our terms of service. Ridiculous interactions are the ones that leave a mark because of how hard I have to beat my brain to lower my IQ when dealing with them. But most calls are nice. I'd say we get more cordial and friendly calls than weird and anger-inducing ones. On average, I get one angry, insulting user once every ten days. The rest of the customers are nice and remain civilised. Some of them are making jokes on the phone and are happy when I call them again to check up on their situation. Once a week, I have a genuinely touching conversation with a user. I'm able to connect with some of these people because I make their lives easier in a way. Users who are stressed are happy to hear that there's a solution to their problem and that I'll be providing it. They thank me dearly and ask about my day… This is touching and important in the time of a pandemic. I'm not seeing anyone outside of my housemates, so I'll take any nice interaction I can have. Moroccan hosts are the best. I wouldn't necessarily have to do anything for them to invite me personally to their hotel or luxurious villa. They like how I sound on the phone and ask for my name so I can be added to their guest list. I'm looking at the pictures of their villa: it looks like a palace. Because of company policies, I can't save the phone number they're giving me to contact them personally, but I appreciate the gesture and end the call with a huge smile on my face.

I am always happy to help customers with their issues. Happy is an overstatement. I'm always willing to help, though. I learn how to reduce my level of vocabulary and syntax to the bare minimum to get my point across. Something I noticed quickly is that customers don't read. If I send an email with more than two sentences, the user won't read it. Let's say the first sentence confirms they have a reservation, and the second sentence indicates how to modify the booking. Nine times out of 10, the user will come back to me asking how to modify the booking. Because of my beloved company rules, I cannot write back 'Can you read?'. Instead, I have to rephrase everything I had already written. The quality agents forbade me from using certain phrases such as 'As mentioned in my previous email' because they are seen as aggressive. I have to spend another minute sending steps I already sent but worded differently. Copy-pasting my previous message is also not something I'm allowed to do. If I could at least tell the user that all of this could've been avoided had they just read the entire email… My hands are tied. Once again.

The day starts like any other. The phone rings at 8:05 a.m., and I immediately regret my life decisions. I get a notification from our team group chat. It's a message from our manager Robert. He's telling us he's leaving the company, and we'll get a new manager to replace him. This is not really a surprise. Since I started, I've seen a handful of managers (not necessarily mine) quit the job. This creates a huge turnover and a lot of changes within teams. If a manager leaves, their team will be merged with another to be supervised by the other team's manager. This doubles the number of employees one manager cares for and disrupts team cohesion. Such restructures are common, and employees are passed on from team to team. Quickly, my team is sending a lot of heartwarming messages.

'We're gonna miss you', 'You were the best manager'.

Are we talking about the same person? I mean, he was nice, but I can count on one hand the times I spoke to my manager, and that includes the 'Hey, how are you?' kind of conversations. I cannot remember anything that he's ever done for us or ever done at all. He was barely there in meetings and spoke for maybe 2 minutes each week. I didn't have to meet with him often. He almost always cancelled the meetings we had scheduled or came in late. He smoked while we were talking, and it looked like he was discovering my metrics when he brought them up. We usually had random conversations about life rather than the job itself. I really liked this managing style. But now he's gone. I couldn't care less, to be honest, but everyone else seemed so affected. Sad emojis, invitations for a drink … they're really going for it. I can't tell if they're sad or just pretending to be. I cannot tell who's being genuine in this corporate world. Everyone speaks as if we're in a dystopian world where all the evilness has suddenly disappeared. All that's left are forced smiles and kind messages. I can get away with being passive-aggressive as long as it comes with a nice emoji. Speaking in a bluntly honest way is not an option.

So, he leaves. OK, we'll be having a new manager then. I hope in the back of my mind that it will be someone nice and funny with whom I can connect and maybe get tips to get a better position shortly. Someone who would help me kick-start my career at this big company. I have high hopes.

I want that, or just someone as unbothered as the first one. I really didn't mind him, and he didn't mind me. It was a great partnership. But really, what I don't want is someone mean. Someone who's constantly on my back and making my life a living hell.

I don't know if my prayers got mixed up that night cause that is exactly what we got.

The next day, we are given the name of our new manager: Doris. I can see some of my colleagues are not happy about this. I asked my colleague Gian why he was making a long face during the meeting.

'She's a snake,' he says. 'My friend had her as a manager, and she made him cry every day until he reported her to HR, and it was not the first time someone did that'.

We have a multi-recidivist on our hands – good. And she's going to be my manager – amazing. I knew people could become famous for being singers or actors, but a terrible manager at a call centre was a new type of reputation I was unfamiliar with. Once the new employee roster is decided, she'll be taking over the people from my team by the end of the week.

We first start with a group meeting. Doris asks everyone to turn on their webcam. She says it's not acceptable not to have it on. And yet she does not have hers turned on. I feel like this is a hostage situation, and my picture is being taken for ransom. There's an underlying tension in the meeting. No one dares to speak. With the previous manager, we would at least attempt to joke around. It was never funny, but it was not heavy like this. Doris introduces herself. She goes straight to the point: she's focused on metrics. The best metrics she can get. She says she will do her best to make this team, my team, the number 1 in the company. She's very competitive, and she wants us to succeed.

I spent enough time in Blue to know that success comes with a price. A price I'll pay with my sanity. She makes a point that none of us should be late and that we should review a book of conduct she wrote because she is all-knowing after all these years working for Blue. I chuckle nervously as I look at my reflection on the screen. It feels like when Dolores Umbridge from the Harry Potter saga takes over Hogwarts. We all know that we're in for a ride. She ends the meeting quickly after she notices that no one interacts. Later, she sends an invitation to meet each team member individually over a few weeks. My date is set up. I accept the invitation.

My time finally comes. This is our first meeting together. The plan is simple: I need her to like me. She joins the meeting. My webcam is turned on, but hers isn't. This is my moment now. I'm doing everything I can to be as nice and fun as possible. If I was a people pleaser before, I certainly evolved into a skilled hypocrite now. Talking to customers the entire day significantly improved my ability to tell people what they want to hear so I can get them to like me. During calls with customers, it was so they could leave me alone faster. During calls with my manager, it was so she could like me enough not to become her personal punching ball. I put on a show. It's scary how good I became at this. I smile from ear to ear, laugh at everything she says, and show interest in what she tells me. And the worst part of this is that it actually works. She's asking me to help her figure out how to do things on our platform. She's a bit rusty, she says. She does not mention why it's been a while since she hasn't been working and definitely does not address the harassment rumours about her. For now, I don't care; I show her. I feel great; not only does she not dislike me, but she trusts me enough to ask for my assistance. Am I her number 2? I'm like a kid desperately trying to become the teacher's favourite. The things I do to get peace at work…

Because we work from home, the company must ensure we're actually working. This comes in the form of various twisted methods to spy on us. We have 'statuses' to select on our system to let the company know what we do at any given time. For example, we can be 'Available' or on 'Break', 'Lunch', in a 'Meeting', etc. This is standard practice, and it does not shock me. But Doris takes it a step further. She creates a group chat in which we have to write what status we're changing to the moment we're changing it. If we go on the 'Lunch' status at 12:00 p.m., we have to write in our group chat 'Lunch' to notify her that we're changing status. Since the system already registers the status change, I fail to understand how this is useful. She has access to this information, so why does she want us to message the whole team whenever we go on a lunch break? To push the vice a bit further, she asks us to write in the group chat whenever we're back from lunch to make sure we're not taking a minute more than we should. In fact, it is advised to return earlier than expected so as not to be late when switching from 'Lunch' to 'Available' again. Every second counts, and if I take 31 minutes instead of the 30 minutes I'm given to eat, I'll get an unpleasant conversation with her. Doris takes an evil pleasure in surveillance. Her demands are becoming more authoritarian by the day, and she takes a whole new turn the day she asks us to write in the group chat when we go to the toilet. Our team seems to use the status 'Break' a lot more than she likes. We're given two breaks of 15 minutes each day, but legally, we can take an additional 15 minutes that we can divide throughout the day if we need to smoke a cigarette or go to the bathroom. These extra 15 minutes were never mentioned during the training. It is an unwritten rule passed by colleagues working here before us, who kindly shared the tip. Doris knows that we know and does not seem happy about it. In an attempt to boost the stats of her team, she wants the 'Break' status time to be as low as possible. To do that, she demands that we inform herself and the entire team when we go to the toilet and return. This is infantilising and humiliating. Not only is she pressuring us to spend as little time as we can in the bathroom, but we also have to let all of our colleagues know how long it took us to flush. I feel like my privacy has been invaded, even though I'm in my own house. When I read the message in which she asks us to do it, I feel like I'm dreaming. Actually, it's more like I'm in a nightmare. I have the disturbing sensation that someone is behind my chair at all times, with their head over my shoulder, making sure I utilise every single second of my existence to devote my soul to this job. It's not a pleasant feeling. I don't do anything because I want to but because I feel pressured. I wait a few minutes before I realise that all my colleagues are obliging. They're each writing their status change in the group chat. I can't go to war on my own, so I do it, too. I feel shame. I don't even go to the toilet anymore. I thought it was one of the advantages of working from home that I could go anytime. Now, I don't dare to step outside my bedroom for fear that I could miss a call and enrage my manager. Every single thing she can monitor, she does. I wonder if she can tell when I'm sneezing. I became paranoid and unplugged my webcam. I message her at 10:15 when I'm going on my 15-minute break and at 10:28 when I come back. I reduce my break by 2 minutes, hoping it makes her happy. A lot of us are doing this. We don't want to be on her radar. We know that if we do not follow her dictatorship, we will get in trouble.

The Doris situation made me nerve-wracking. The same applies to my teammates, who feel a strong urge to go out every night at the pub to dish out what they have. We meet at the pub regularly. It's more a need than anything else at this point. It's the only moment of joy I have during the day. I'm meeting with people who understand what I'm going through and whom I can talk to. As I walk into the pub, I don't even have time to take off my coat; we're starting to complain about Doris. It's not just Doris, it's also Blue and the customers. It's everything. I was once a shy and quiet girl, but that's no longer the case. I jump on any occasion I have to trash talk about this job and anything related to it. I enjoy it; it feels cathartic. I order a pint and come back to the table running. I don't want to miss a single thing they're saying. We go around the table and share our experiences with Doris. Everyone has something to say. We all had unpleasant situations with her, some of us more than others. I did, too. But I also had nice moments. I don't share these. It's not the right time and place. We're here to demolish our management, and no nuances are allowed. It's a blast. I can't stop laughing. I gasp whenever I learn new information about Doris or how messed up someone else's situation is. It's an emotional rollercoaster. It's a change from the robotic mindset I adopt every day. For once I'm using my brain a little bit. It's for social activities, not sudokus, but it still feels nice. When it's my turn, I make sure to detail every second of the tiniest moments I've had with Doris. I continued with customers' stories, such as how angry they made me or how stupid they were. I don't mention the nice ones, either. This isn't coffee time; it's an evening at the pub. As I'm about to finish my story, I notice that my glass is empty. A colleague offers to buy me a second pint. I hesitate. I had never drunk two in one night before. But I don't want to stop now; I feel like I have so much more to say. I accepted, and he came back with pints full of beers for a few of us at the table. It's at this time that I notice that everyone has already drunk a few. I never cared before, but it's true they often have a few drinks ahead of me. We continue our discussions until late in the night. I go home feeling satisfied that I emptied my emotional bag, and I go to bed knowing that the following day, I will fill it up again. I am almost looking forward to it. That way, I will have an excuse to go out and complain about it more.

As the week passes, I become fascinated by Doris. She's the topic of every conversation; she leaves no one indifferent. Most of my colleagues hate her. They become inspired when it comes to creating new insults to qualify her. I'm intrigued by this person. I wonder if she really is as awful as she comes across at work. I want to meet her face-to-face. Meeting someone is difficult while on a lockdown, but since we can already go to the pub, we can also easily go for a coffee outside in the parks. My friend Jenna and I, clearly her favourites, offer to meet one day when our schedules align. She accepts. When the day arrives, she cancels last minute and says she is too nervous to meet. I miss my chance to finally befriend an Irish person.

I didn't mean to make her nervous. In fact, before she sent me that message, I didn't know that it was an emotion she could feel. She was making me nervous every day. And the whole team as well. She terrorises dozens of people at work on a daily basis but is too nervous to meet outside for a coffee. I began to make theories about her life and what it could be. Maybe she has anger issues and found that this job is the perfect way to mentally torture others so she does not have to torture herself. Perhaps she's sadistic. Maybe she's kind and does not realise how she treats people. Knowing she was nervous created a whole new reality for me. This person has layers. She's not only a pixelated monster which inspires resignation letters. She knows fear, like the rest of us humans.

I'm still afraid of her, though. I want to stay out of trouble.

The trouble is translating to a 'Strike', which I can receive for various reasons. Having a strike on my professional record comes with a lot of consequences. The main one is that I'm ineligible for a performance bonus after 3 strikes. If, by some miracle, I manage to get a bonus, it can be taken away from me because of an unrelated mistake. The third strike agents get on their employees' files means placing them in a special program. It's called a preparation program, and it is designed to provide some additional training to the agent to make sure they're up to speed with the job and won't get any new strikes going forward. In reality, this program is a Damocles' sword above the agent's head. They're given a few months to improve in terms of stats, quality of work, and compliance with the company's rules. If no improvement is noticed, they will be let go. While on that program, they're also ineligible for any bonuses. What is being depicted as an accompaniment to fix one agent's work is, in reality, a scheme to push them off a cliff and get rid of them, either by firing them for poor performances or because the pressure put on the agent will be so tough they will quit on their own. Some excellent agents can also be affected. Strikes are ruthless and override any good work that's being done. Let's say I solve 100 cases a week, but I forget to write some notes about a conversation with a customer in one of them: I get a strike. If I get a 100% customer satisfaction score, but I forget to tell the customer their call is being recorded, I get a strike.

My day is divided into several parts. Ninety percent of it is answering calls and emails. Sometimes, I have meetings. I have two breaks of 15 minutes and one lunch break of 30 minutes. The lunch break is infamous for being too short, and although many companies have that same 30-minute break, it remains abnormally short for any well-conceived individual. We're not allowed to start preparing our lunch before our lunch break. They will notice if we do. We must wait until the break starts to prepare, eat and digest our food. This is not enough to do all of it, and I always go back to work with my heart in my throat because I ingest my food so quickly. I also can't eat anything too healthy either. Most of my meals are food that I preheated or processed food that I microwave. I don't have the energy to meal prep after a long shift, and I can't anticipate when my day will start too long in advance. Depending on when I start my day, I have to eat at different times. My lunch break is also set for me; I can't choose when I can have it. Sometimes I don't have lunch. Sometimes, I have dinner around midnight. My body is having a hard time following this schedule. I complain about it to some of my colleagues.

'This is the same in most companies,' they say.

I know, but it still does not make it OK. I'm sure any dietitian would agree. It was said during my interview that the schedule I'd have to follow would change every week. I can work any day of the week; the weekends are included, as well as typical holidays such as Christmas because Santa Claus obviously needs to book a room after his night of hard labour. When I check my schedule, I see that I'm meant to work that day. I find it underwhelming, but I signed up for this, so I don't have a choice. I log in to work my shift. I reply to a few emails from the day before and wait until someone contacts me. 15 minutes pass, and I don't get a new email or a phone call. This is new to me; I never even knew this could happen. Silence. Not a single thing to disturb me. I might as well walk out of my room and enjoy Christmas Day since no one seems to be contacting us today. That would be way too easy for me, and Blue obviously isn't going to let me off the hook so easily. They are systems to measure how productive we all are as agents: how long we spend on a case, etc. When we don't have a case, that timer is still running and measuring how much we're actively trying to have a case. Unlike calls, emails aren't forwarded to agents automatically. We have to pick them up from what we call a queue, essentially where all emails sent to us would be. That queue is usually full since someone is always contacting us. For reasons that are obvious to everyone but Blue, there aren't any emails in the queue on Christmas Day. I wonder what people are up to on that day; it's really hard to tell. Picking up a case is not possible, and yet, because it is what I have to do, I have to try and pick up an email from an empty queue. The systems record my clicks and the time I spend on the screen, in the queue, and clicking in the void to prove that I'm actively trying to get a case and work. Failing to do so reduces my productivity statistics, which will get me an unpleasant conversation with Doris and a strike, and this is not what I want as a Christmas gift. Against my better instincts and my common sense, I oblige, and I spend 8 hours during Christmas clicking on an empty screen to satisfy the measurements of a robot. The metrics measured today will be my productivity time and will be the direct results of how much and how long I clicked for, just to get an email that never arrived. I don't think anyone has ever had the worst

Christmas in history. Or perhaps Anne Frank did. But she didn't celebrate Christmas.

A week later, I had a meeting with Doris. It's my performance review. She shows me all of my numbers on a graphic. They're right next to my team's average score. She noticed that on the 25th of December, I did not resolve any case. She asks me why. I laugh at first; I think she's joking. I understand she's not when I don't hear her laugh back. I can't believe she's serious. Is she really asking me why I didn't receive a single call during Christmas? Should I explain why no one called customer support that day? I want to smash my head against my keyboard. How much damage will it do to my brain? It can't be worse than having this conversation. I told her that no one contacted our support on that day, possibly because it is a Holiday celebrated worldwide.

'Humph…' I can hear.

She's not convinced. She types in on the report, 'Agent says they didn't receive calls that day'. I wonder who's going to read this note. The manager of her manager? I wonder if any of them has the tiniest sense of logic to be reading this and thinking it makes sense. Furthermore, they can see that I spent my entire 8-hour shift clicking on the queue to get a case and that there simply weren't any emails sent to us that day. They also measure how many emails are sent by customers each day. They have enough numbers to understand what was going on during Christmas. Why can't they put two and two together? I feel like I'm taking crazy pills at this point. I have always felt like the sanest person in this company, and yet I'm turning crazier by the minute. I guess having to explain simple concepts to stupid people has that effect. The meeting ends, and I look at the wall in front of me for a solid 10 minutes. I wonder what my life has become.

I never had a manager always lurking in the back, watching me, spying on me, hoping I would commit a mistake so they could immediately hammer me with it. Thanks to these ingenious systems put in place to track every single one of my movements, they can tell if I'm online, clicking, typing, searching for a way to end my misery on Google or worse than everything: not being productive. There are 3 types of metrics, which are all equally twisted:

The satisfaction bonus is the first, and it's devilishly genius. There are 2 satisfaction scores that a customer can leave after an interaction with our support. They rate how satisfied they are with the company and how happy they are with the agent who took their call. The ranking system works as follows:

If I get between 9 and 10, this is considered a good score, and I will get a point.

Between 7 and 8 is considered a passive score, so 0.

A score between 1 and 6 is a negative score, taking away from my points. The lower I am, the lower I lose points.

If I get the following scores: 1×10, 3×8 and 1×1, my score will be negative, and I will not receive the bonus. Though 4 customers are happy with me, 3 of them did not leave a high enough score for me to receive points, and one of them left me a 1/10, which negates all the good that a 10/10 does. Angry customers who were denied a refund request often leave bad scores and want to blame both the company and the agent. These metrics are far from being accurate and designed to make us fail. A customer leaving an 8/10 might think they gave me a good score. In reality, it would have the same effect not to vote at all. A bad note is also three times stronger than a good one. Having 3 scores of 10/10 and one score of 0/10 makes my result neutral because of how impactful one bad review is. Needless to say, with a neutral score, I cannot get a satisfaction bonus. As a matter of fact, I need 8 good reviews to compensate for one terrible one. This notation system is called NPS. In my previous company, we used the CSAT system, which let people rate agents from 0 to 5, but the principle remains the same. It's a one-sided, twisted way of calculating an agent's work and progress towards an unreachable goal. I'd have more success asking people to smile at a funeral home.

—The second important metric is the number of cases we solve weekly. During a pandemic, it is hard to get high numbers when working in a call centre specialising in holiday rentals. This is like asking an ice cream shop to perform as well in December as they do in June. We obviously are always under the target that was set because of the low volumes of calls. When there are many more calls tough, that target is being raised to ensure we still don't reach it. Even if we manage the impossible for a week, we have to repeat the effort throughout the month for it to even count. The average monthly performance is what matters here.

—The last and probably the worst is the one we're calling 'Handling time'. Not content to know how many cases I can solve in a week, the employer also wants to know how long it takes for me to solve them. Our average handling time is around 8 minutes for emails and 15 minutes for phone calls. At first, these seemed easily reachable targets. Let's say a customer emails me about a refund request. Denying it probably won't take more than 3 minutes. So, I'm golden. I have 5 minutes to myself now. But it becomes tricky when I need more than eight minutes to figure out what's going on. If the problem is so complex, I need 10 minutes to at least understand it. Ten more minutes to try and do some research before I realise there's nothing useful in the help articles I have access to. Then another 10 minutes to message my colleagues, who are using up this precious time to try and help me to no avail. I just wasted 30 minutes, and I have no solution to offer, no clue where to begin my searches, and yet I have to answer this customer. This can quickly turn into a one-hour case since making things up as I write to make my email look more prominent is a skill that takes time. And the same will happen once that customer comes back to me because I still didn't provide any solution. The best thing to do in these situations is to ask for lots of details, screenshots, timeframes, and anything that might make the customer not want to answer me because it's too much to provide. I cross my fingers each time I have a similar situation. *Please don't come back.* It takes an hour for me to get rid of some cases. This is not going to go unnoticed. Every time I take more time than I should to solve a case, a timer turns red on my screen and sends an alert to the system to signal how slow I am at the job. The timer starts once I receive the email and stays in a neutral colour as long as I'm under 8 minutes. After that, the timer turns red, and the more time I take, the bigger the hole I'm digging myself into becomes. These cases are then reviewed by supervisors who will judge if the time I took on this case was necessary. If the supervisor, who has virtually no idea how to do my job, says this issue shouldn't take that long, then this is final. There's no use in protesting. Most of the time in this job, whenever a manager tells me that I did something wrong, this is a divine word. It can't be changed. It can't be challenged. I messed up, and that's it. Even if I do have a good case for myself, if I explain and defend myself, I still won't change anyone's mind. These words aren't the words of the person delivering them to me. It comes from higher-ups whom I've never met and simply saw the 1-hour red mark on my performance report. That's also a good way to judge a manager's work ethic. If they start by showing empathy, telling me they understand this is difficult … But that their manager wants me to do this and that, then I know that they only mean to help. They want them to get off my back because it means they'll get off their own back, too.

Now, if my manager breaks down the news and takes sadistic pleasure in doing so, it means that I'm unfortunately being managed by a sociopath. That's the situation I'm in.

I am lucky that Doris has a soft spot for me. I'm witnessing how she treats some of my colleagues, and it's disturbing, to say the least. She has set new targets for us, and we have to call 50 users a week, as requested by the company. I need to call people daily because they request it or because fixing an issue over the phone is much faster than writing a long and complicated email. 50 calls a week sounds like a lot to me. We're talking about outbound calls, meaning calls we initiate, not calls we receive. My friend Coralie had a week with 27 outbound calls. A solid score but not enough for Stalin. The response was immediate: a coaching meeting where Doris specifically asked Coralie to make more phone calls if she did not want to get a strike on her record.

Coralie decides to take the challenge. She's been in the company long enough to understand that there's no use in fighting back. The company wants her to make more calls, but Doris will not let it go. How she achieved that during a time when the volume of cases was low because of the pandemic is quite funny. Coralie called users to ask them if they were alright. Users who did not need any additional help or did not request a phone call. She simply asked if there was anything Blue could do for them at the moment or if, since the last time they got in touch with us, they needed additional support. The customers' reactions were wholesome. During the pandemic, most of them were pleasantly surprised by the gesture. If this occurred any other time, people would probably ask to be left alone. They didn't know, of course, that this was the result of an oppressing dictator's policy. This made the interactions a lot nicer than they were usually because when there is no problem to fix, there usually isn't any room for conflict to grow. She spent the whole week calling user after user, making sure they didn't need anything from her. Some calls lasted 2 minutes, while others lasted half an hour because some retired people liked to talk and felt alone during the lockdown. This resulted in Coralie's best week yet: 134 outbound calls. More than double the target we were given by Doris. She was proud and expected our manager to praise her for her hard work. The following Monday, the team numbers were given. As usual, Doris shares each agent's stats in a group chat where everyone can see them. This is another twisted trick that makes us compete with each other. That way, she can make sure everyone knows who the least performing agent is. She also does not care to add if that person was on sick leave or had personal problems. She cares about the numbers and knows we don't want to be at the bottom of the list. She points out the 134-call Coralie made, and instead of congratulating her, she scolds her.

'We need to ensure we're not exaggerating the outbound phone calls', she declares.

I laugh. This is why we can never win in this company.

Doris set these expectations, and someone finally reached them. In old Doris fashion, she cannot be happy for one of her team members. She prefers to bring them down publicly and destroy the tiny feeling of accomplishment we all get each week after sweating blood and tears for 40 hours.

There are fewer cases than there needs to be to make 50 outbound calls. No one can leave their house, so no one can travel and rent anything on our platform at the moment. We get maybe 30 tickets a week. This means that unless we call each person twice within that week, we won't reach the target of outbound calls. Calling someone twice is already exaggerating the outbound phone calls. If we're not doing it, we're not doing enough. If we're doing it, we're doing too much. We can never win with them. They have a hard time understanding that these metrics are the direct results of interactions with people. We can't have a perfectly round number when the influx of contacts depends on the current state of the world. And we're on lockdown, for Christ's sake. This is a perfect example of how she is treating the team members she doesn't like. I've had trouble reaching out about my targets sometimes, and I've never received any comments about them.

A lot of big companies have their headquarters in Ireland. The main reason is the interestingly low tax rate they have to pay each year. When I talk to people, it's commonly said that some don't even pay taxes. I'm not sure how this works, and I'm not sure that I care. I'm having a hard time understanding why they're hiring people in Ireland, though. It's the country with one of the highest minimum salaries in Europe. Surely, they could hire people in Italy for half of the price or in Romania for a tenth of it. I could never figure out why they would waste money employing unqualified people for customer support in a country where the salary was €1,800 minimum. There must've been a reason. Some shady secret deals with the government gave them subventions the more contracts they created. And they must create a hell of a lot. Most of the people working in call centres tend to quit after only a few months. This means that the recruiting process never ends, as there is a constant need to find new blood to sacrifice for these million-dollar companies. According to the research I've done, the more an Irish company creates jobs, the more they can benefit from various tax incentives like reduced corporate tax rates or tax credits for hiring. Although I cannot confirm this theory for certain, this sounds like the most rational explanation to me. I can't find any other reason why a company would be so inclined to hire so many people on permanent contracts if they knew that these employees would not last more than 6 months. I'm also not naive enough to believe they're doing this for the economy. And that would explain why they're willing to pay Irish salaries, plus bonuses.

Ah … The bonuses … They made the base salary look much bigger, and we were promised bonuses which could add up to €500. What are the conditions for being entitled to receive these high amounts of money? As mentioned, a bonus is based on an agent's performance. For example, I get a bonus if I get a customer satisfaction score of 80% or above. I noticed now that these scores are difficult to achieve and sometimes even impossible. I cannot satisfy customers if I deny their refund requests, for example. The company does not want me to refund the customer; I have to deliver the news, and I get a bad score. It's as simple as that. I will never receive any of these bonuses.

Bonuses are so difficult to obtain, so why are agents still hoping to get one? For economic reasons, of course. Since the beginning of this job, all of my colleagues and I have found ourselves in a delicate financial state, all because of a bureaucratic impairment called the 'Emergency tax'. To work in Ireland, I must apply for a social security number. To apply for one, I have to have a job, meaning I can only apply once I start my job. The process to obtain a social security number is abnormally slow; it can take up to 3 months, and because of Covid, this can even take longer. Without a social security number, employees receive only half of their salary until they can provide a number to the payroll. The state puts the other half on hold, which will give it back once the employee receives their number. Most of us came to Ireland with some savings, but savings do go away, especially when I make less than what I was promised and only get half of that lower estimation each month. My team works relentlessly like hamsters on flamed wheels to meet unrealistic expectations so that we can get an extra 50 euros on our paycheck. This is how much one bonus is worth: 50

euros. We were promised much more when they made us believe we could get more than one in a month. We can't even get one in a year. But after 4 months in this emergency situation, even a 50 euro bonus makes a difference. The combined stress of the financial pressure, added on top of the need to perform, starts to break spirits, and most of us become nerve-wracking. Although Blue is not responsible for it, they did not warn us that this could happen. Some companies take care of the administrative aspect when hiring people, especially from abroad, since employees don't have bureaucratic knowledge overseas. Blue isn't one of them. The emergency tax has been a recurring problem for employees before us and continues to be for newcomers. I would've liked it if, before asking me to change countries for their company, Blue could have mentioned the potentiality of not being paid in full for a few months. They're also not providing any support in the situation, and they completely detach themselves from it. They're saying it's not their fault, which is technically correct. But it's still handled in a bad fashion. We all learned about the emergency tax when receiving our first paycheck, so not only did they not mention it before we signed the contract, but they also kept it a secret for 30 days before the first paycheck was issued. It's also worth noting that we must ask for an explanation, as they sent the document without any note. For some employees, the financial situation in which they find themselves is too big to get out of. Some of us have to leave the country and go back to our parents' houses because they cannot keep up with the cost of living while being paid so little. To Blue, this is not a problem. They're the ones quitting, so they don't have to pay them any compensation, and they will be hiring someone else in the following days, which means more contracts will be created for fewer taxes paid. It's a win-win situation.

The Covid restrictions are starting to be lifted, so my colleagues and I can meet again in the city. Although we're in a difficult financial situation, we still meet at the pub. It feels like group therapy more than anything else. I ordered my first pint and went into autopilot mode. I'm sharing lengthy complaints about every single thing I can think of. The mouse I'm using, the brightness of my computer, Doris again. I'm even rehashing old discussions I didn't detail enough. When I'm done talking, I order another pint and return to the table to listen to my colleagues do the same. We don't react the same way anymore. Nothing shocks us. We mostly stare at the table, nodding and agreeing with what's being said. We don't really laugh all that much. I think we all feel lonely and are emotionally dependent on each other. This job isolates us and is mentally demanding. We must know that we have an escape at the end of the day, or it'll be too much to bear. At no point did we talk about quitting. It's a toxic relationship that we have. We log in to work every day to receive abuse from both customers and Blue, all so that we can share our trauma at night with our colleagues who experience the same. It's a reassuring thought but not a healthy one. We need the job because we have bills to pay. We have bills to pay because we're here to work.

After hours of repetitions, the barman comes to our table and announces that the pub will be closing soon. We order one last drink, and we all head home. I come back to my apartment, and I quickly get into bed. I stare at my computer. It's unplugged. It can't harm me for now. But it's still in my room with me. The moment it turns on is the moment I'm going to receive abuse from it. I turned my back to it and checked my phone. I received a notification from my bank informing me of my daily spending. I ordered 4 pints today. It's more than what I could've drunk a few months ago. It's still less than my colleagues, though this does not really comfort me. I'm not sure if we're emotionally dependent on each other or dependent on alcohol. We're all triggered by the same thing, though. The one thing I'm turning my back to until I have to face it again the next day.

This is concerning to me. I talk to some of my colleagues about it. I met some people from the Spanish team, and I asked them if they had experienced similar situations. They laugh at me. Not only are they completely aware of their own alcohol consumption, but they are also quite fond of a white powder that can be taken from the nose. I'm taken aback. And yet, I'm not really surprised. *That's how everyone can get through their day,* I thought. This does not seem to bother them all that much. This is one of these job requirements, I suppose. When they invite me to their parties, they have lines ready on the kitchen table. How can they all get such important quantities? After all, this is Ireland. Importing this is quite difficult and expensive. When

I asked, they told me not to spread the word. They tell me that someone could lose their job if they get found out. It's when they mention the name of their dealer that I understand that they got it from a manager.

I get a call one day, and it's a guy who starts the call as follows:

— 'Yeah … hum … my booking hum … you charged me for it.'

I'm reviewing his account, and he booked a hotel room today.

— 'Yes, we did charge you; the reservation started at 3 p.m.', I informed him.

— 'I'm not at the hotel, and I'm not going to, so you can cancel it and refund me.'

It's the no-refund policy. I have to crush his dreams.

— 'I reviewed the hotel policy.' I continue. 'Unfortunately, they do not allow refunds for no show-ups.'

— 'I had to do business elsewhere, and you guys never confirmed the booking with me, so you messed it up.'

This guy forgot he made a booking, and now it's our fault.

— 'We usually send reminders via email. Did you get them?' I ask.

Of course, he did. He checks his inbox and sees the reminders.

— 'Okay, so it's both our fault', he continues. 'I'd say 60% yours and 40% mine, oh well, maybe 30%. So just refund me, and let's be done with it.'

I laugh. My brain is filled with words I want to say but cannot. But I have to decline professionally and use a friendly tone to make sure the quality agents don't come down on me for not sounding too enthusiastic. I have to repeat myself 3 times until he finally gives up. This is not a violent confrontation, but it feels mentally exhausting. Rephrasing the same thing over and over must be frying my brain cells, as I feel less alive each time I hang up a similar call. Thankfully, there's one thing I'm grateful for: I have some after-call time. When I finish an inbound call, I'm given 5 minutes to work on my case. This is to write a recap of my conversation with the customer to document the case. It also gives me time to write an email to the user, which is mandatory even though we just called seconds ago. They need to have a written statement of what we discussed. During this after call time, I cannot get another phone call. If a call comes through, it will be directed to another available agent. I'm not considered available when I'm on the after-call status. After 5 minutes, I automatically become available again and can receive a phone call right away if there's one waiting for me. This happened a lot during the second lockdown announcement. Five minutes can go fast, so it's easier to take notes as I'm making the call to take the least amount of time possible after hanging up. It's also best to remember everything I mentioned during the call since this will also be a strike on my quality review. Each detail has to be documented; even if the customer asked me what time it was, it needs to be put in writing. If I'm not done wrapping up my email after the 5 minutes I have, I can get a phone call, leaving my case hanging only to build up more work as I'll have to go through it all over again later. When getting call after call, I find myself having to come back to cases I had an hour ago to finish my notes. One hour is enough to forget which case was which and what I talked about on the phone. It is also commonly not well seen to stay for too long on the after-call status. Because I cannot receive a phone call during that time, I am not considered 'productive', and the larger the amount of time I spend under that status, the lazier I am in the eyes of my manager. It is believed that the time is used to take a break between calls rather than what it actually should be used for, which is to document a case. During quiet times, we're asked to quit the status as soon as we hang up the call to make our stats look nicer. If the company thinks we're available 24/7, they'll be happy. We oblige, of course, because we're dogs on a leash.

The next day, I received a complicated phone call involving several users. The call takes an hour. I have to document the case properly and send 3 follow-up emails to 3 different customers. The 5 minutes of after-call I have is not enough, and I know that another call is waiting for me since it's 10 p.m. and most agents are offline at that time. I cannot be available again, so I need time to finish this. I decided to manually set my status after-call and use it for 8 minutes instead of 5 to make sure I'm not missing out on anything in my notes (which could get me in trouble if I did). I receive a notification. It's a message from someone I do not know. I open the message. 'Put your status on available. You've been on after-call for 8 minutes. No hello. No, thank you. Someone that I never met has ordered me to change my status because I spent 3 extra minutes documenting my case. Not only is proper documentation a requirement in this job, but if I don't do it correctly for such a complex issue, my colleagues will never understand what is going on. This issue involves 3 users, and it is likely that one of them will call back and they might not get me on the line. If they get a colleague of mine, they need to know what was said and done before. I need time to put this in writing in 3 different cases on top of sending 3 different emails. This message feels like a whip cracking on my back. I'm an adult working for one of the richest companies in the world, and I feel like I'm in a coal mine, being asked to mine faster. I know what this person wants; they want me to become available because staying too long on 'after-call' will not look good for the manager of the manager of my manager. They also want me to be perfectly complying with their overly demanding quality standard in less time than is needed to microwave popcorn. I cannot win. Whatever I choose to do, I will be in the wrong here. If I take another phone call right now and the issue is just as complex as the previous one, I will mix everything up and forget my previous conversation. And as a result, I panic. I'm shaking because of how nervous this message made me. I have trouble typing in; my screen is becoming blurry. My eyes water because I want to cry, but if I have a panic attack now, it'll only be worse. I have to keep going and finish this. I write as fast as I can and make many typos. The timer is turning dark red, and that message is still here. I read myself out loud to make sure my message makes sense. I feel like a gun is being pointed at me. I scratch the back of my right hand with my left fingers and switch sides when my skin turns red and burns. I'm biting my lips and bouncing my legs up and down because of how stressed I am. If I were in an office, maybe someone would come up and calm me down. It's not that serious. The isolation and the tactics employed by the company make this a lot worse than it needs to be.

I'm not taking the time to realise how absurd and wrong it is to have someone monitor me in real time and talk to me that way. Surely, that person could take the next phone call if customer care was their preoccupation. But only numbers matter to them. Numbers I provide. I need to be on all fronts without committing a single mistake. I mustn't have any metric number in the red on my performance report, and my documentation notes need to be perfect. There's a cost to this, and this cost is my sanity. I'm swallowing blood after biting my lips too hard and putting myself on available again after 10 minutes and 23 seconds. Another call picks up automatically, and I start all over again.

I decided to take some time off. Not to go on vacation; I'm not going anywhere. I'm staying at home, but I'm just unable to log in today to work. Calling in sick would probably be more appropriate, but if I do this, I won't get paid. So, I use my holiday balance to take mental rest instead. What a concept. I reflect on my situation and what happened over the last few months. It felt like a tornado. A vortex which had sucked me in and from which I couldn't escape. I wake up some nights sweating, hearing the sound of the phone ringing. Sometimes, I wake up thinking I forgot to call someone back. The job is not leaving me once I clock out, and it doesn't feel like 40 hours a week but a 24/7 job. My life revolves around it. All that I can talk about is the job. I am talking about it with my friends, who are also my colleagues. We cannot talk about anything else. For hours, we tell each other what our days were like, what types of calls we got, which customers were the most annoying, and how the metrics are designed to make our nerves wrack. We can discuss it for hours, and it wouldn't occur to us that we had no other conversation topic.

On the night of that day off, I invited some colleagues over. One of them already left the company. She points out several times how similar we sound to a broken record, mentioning the same things over and over again. She is right. This job is draining us. It slowly turns us psychotic, and we need to evacuate all the stress we built up. It is cathartic but also reassuring to know that we aren't the only ones to lose our minds. Ironically, these obsessive conversations are the only way to remain sane. And just as ironically, on my day off I keep talking about my job.

It affects all of us. I can see the job's effects on our sanity, but I can also see how our bodies change. The demeanour on our faces, how we gain weight for lack of physical activity. Whether it is intended or not, this job drains us and sucks the life out of us. It's a never-ending cycle of conflict. It comes from the customers and from the management. I'm cornered. If I want to please the customers and give them what they want, I will not satisfy my manager. If I want to make my manager happy, I have to follow the guidelines which are enraging the customer. I can never win. I'm trapped inside this endless loop of misery, and I'm not really seeing a way out. The expectations set for me are more difficult each week, and I'm reaching a breaking point. Waking up to turn on the computer is physically painful. I can feel it in my stomach. I feel this weight every time the phone rings, wondering if this is a customer who's going to threaten to find and kill me. I feel it when my manager tells me that I'm not doing enough, even though I'm losing hair over the stress of the job and how much work I'm already giving. Whatever I do, it won't be enough. The pressure crushing us is real, and when we bring it up with Doris, she says that we should take it slower and breathe. Taking it slower is not an option since Doris herself insists on performing to the best of our ability. The breathing part is a bit easier, but I've already been doing that since the day I was born, and it didn't make my neurosis better. The mental support provided by the company is simply non-existent. They say that they're able to offer psychological help and sessions with therapists. They never get into the specifics, and I'm not sure anyone ever requested an appointment. After all, I don't necessarily wish to complain about the company to the company. I'm sure Snow White wouldn't book a therapy session with her stepmother to complain about how much anxiety she gets from being threatened with being killed every day (by her). In a nutshell, that help is just wind. I am sent the number of a suicide hotline by a colleague when I mention that I'm having a really hard time. It's extremely comical and sad at the same time, and I'm not sure what to do with it. It would be better to have private therapy sessions covered, but that would require company benefits, and our contract is stripped of any. I'm longing for the day this becomes a legal requirement for any customer support job. I don't know anyone who works in that field who's not actively needing help. I think we should all go to therapy. The customers, my colleagues and my manager. Especially her.

A lot of my colleagues can no longer bear the situation with Doris. We're exhausted and cannot keep up with her unrealistic expectations. She's more demanding each week and never has a kind word for any work done. If I'm good in one area, she won't congratulate me. Instead, she will point out that I am not doing as well in all the other areas of my job. I learned how to roll with it, but this affects some of my teammates more than others, and rightfully so. We all work hard, and even if there's an area for improvement, we need the feel to hear words of encouragement from time to time. The pressure of the job and the lack of recognition make it hard to finish the week without feeling angry and disappointed. We want to do well, but this is too hard. We can never win no matter what we do.

Several of my colleagues try to rebel against Doris. They tell her they don't like her management style and that she's breaking us down instead of building us up. When she hears this, Doris cries. She sobs and asks why no one likes her. It's not clear if this is another one of her tactics or a cry for help. I'm wondering if her managers know about this and if they plan to do something to help. Whenever there is a situation with her, they usually don't intervene that much. Reports to HR aren't doing much either. I don't think anyone cares to help her, to be honest. The agents she terrorises on a daily basis certainly won't help. We're all numb to most human emotions at this point. Her management doesn't seem to care. It's nice to know that at least we share the same misfortune of being managed by psychopaths.

I try to enjoy my time off as much as I can. I spend 2 weeks doing nothing. I'm due to start working again on the next week. The day before I have to come back, I turn on my computer to check my schedule. I need to know at what time I'll be starting on the following day. I couldn't have known before because the scheduling team does not plan too far ahead. I have no choice but to log on to my computer during my time off to know when I'll start again. I'll be starting at 8 a.m. Noted. A week later, Doris asked me to jump on a call with her. When I join, she tells me that she'll be giving me a strike because I used the computer outside of my working hours. I'm not meant to do that. I should only be using the computer for work-related purposes. I'm speechless once again. I tell her that I understand. I don't have the strength to drag common sense into this conversation. I wish I could be on holiday again.

The idea to get a promotion was the Eldorado for us. The promise that we would get a promotion into a higher department, where no phone calls would go through. A department solely operating via email, and from Monday to Tuesday. Getting there was more a game of luck than anything else. The recruitment process baffles me. Some really good agents were never promoted, while others, whose work was questionable, got sent off after 1 month to a better place. How does this recruiting process work? Do they just flip a coin and hope it lands on a good employee? Are they aware that they put some despicable managers in charge, making our day a living hell? Maybe this is all going to plan. Maybe they do need someone to terrorise us so we commit as little mistakes as possible.

Like any fairytale losing its magic upon growing up, the myth of a promotion being a good thing gets demystified once I learn about its reality. Unfortunately for her, my friend Coralie gets promoted to a higher department. The promotion cannot be refused. Agents are being sent there when there's a need for people, not to reward hard-working employees. The conditions in this department are even tougher, leading many people to quit. I'm confident in saying this is Blue's intention. Replacements are always needed, and agents are being drafted just like they would have been during World War II. With all these new responsibilities comes an outstanding raise of €50 per month. This department handles pressing issues that are mostly related to cleanliness. This also includes poop-related issues. It really does. There are people who defecate on beds (or anywhere else; it could be the floor or the bathtub…) and leave their room or apartment that they rented to go on about their day without a worry in the world. The host, or the next unlucky guest, has to send a video or a photo of the number two for review. Coralie's job is to look at the beautiful masterpiece they sent and act accordingly. This means a refund. As if this job was not already draining what was left of her soul, she now has the joy of reviewing faeces pictures all day. And it does not stop here! She also has to review clichés of used tampons left on the floor, used condoms on the couch, bed bugs and their eggs under the mattress, and so many other wonderful pictures I can't begin to name them all. It is unfortunate that a human adult who has the right to vote would leave such gifts somewhere they rented. It's even more unfortunate that all of this has to be documented and reviewed by Coralie's poor, innocent eyes for 8 hours a day, 5 days a week. Though the cases she receives aren't as numerous as they were in the other department, they are cut off by conflictual phone calls. It becomes her duty to resolve immediate conflicts between parties. The day starts, and she gets a phone call from a man wanting to cancel the reservation made by a young woman in his apartment. He claims that he saw many men coming into the apartment and leaving 30 minutes later, one after the other. This indicates that shady business is happening behind closed doors: sex business. It's a common issue: sex workers rent someone's place to do their work, and the owner wants them out of there as soon as possible. Agents have to resolve the matter by calling the guest and asking them to leave. This is a delicate situation. There are no tangible proofs that the guest is a sex worker, only assumptions. The host might be right, but the fact remains that the decision to kick out the guest is made on observations and nothing concrete. Upon being promoted, Coralie and the other agents did not receive any relevant training on these topics. They were briefly shown the basics: how to document a case in this new department and which tools they should be using going forward. No relevant training has been provided towards communication. It is expected of them to have proper communication skills, but I don't think any of them ever had to accuse someone of being a prostitute before, let alone in a professional way. They have to call the guest and ask them to leave their rental because it is believed that they're using it for sex work. This is extremely sensitive, and so many things could go wrong here. Proper training should be provided on how to deliver the news, handle reactions and use the correct verbiage. We're talking about already exhausted agents who did not ask to be promoted and aren't given a choice to refuse the change of department. This conflict is moderate compared to other situations that can occur. There are times when the person calling in is in immediate danger: they can be physically threatened or assaulted by the other party or face a situation where the other person does not want to leave. This happened one time: a host would find their guest to be still in their apartments 5 days after the end of their stay. The guest was a 19-year-old teenager bringing a new wave of girls in his pick-up truck every day, only to party and ravage the place. This happened in a small village, and the inhabitants complained about the noise and mess created by the whole situation. The host was powerless and didn't know how what to do. When they contacted Coralie, she urged them to call the police. This is the correct thing to do in this situation, and this is a logical decision. It took 5 days for this host to resort to calling the police. It seems long, but it is because there's an important element that should not be forgotten about: user ratings. If a host cancels a reservation, regardless of whether it is justified, they will be getting a penalty. A strike, if I may, just like us agents! Their listing will get less visibility, they will get fewer bookings, and it might even come down to cancellation fees. In fear of having their reputation sabotaged, most hosts will never cancel their guest's reservations. Instead, they will ask us to mediate the situation or to cancel it ourselves. I'm fascinated by how well-behaved these people are. They're giving away their place so it can be rented on a website, which takes a big commission on each reservation. Yet, they're still hesitating to kick out a guest ravaging their property to protect their online reputation. Did they forget the property is theirs? Hell, I'm kicking out spiders as soon as their web is too big. I understand that some of them use the platform to make a living, but it's baffling that hosts would bend over backwards for Blue. Blue needs them, not the other way around. In my opinion, the power balance is not what it is supposed to be. I'm disgusted that on top of mistreating their employees, Blue also holds the hosts in the palm of their hands, ready to crush them when needed. Without the hosts, we don't have properties to rent, and the whole website can't function. They're Blue's bread maker. Similarly to us, hosts will also get ratings based on their performance: how welcoming they were, how helpful they've been, etc. And just like ours, their notation system is intransigent. It has to be 5 stars. It cannot be less. Four stars are not considered a good score and will affect their score negatively. Some guests innocently leave a 4-star review because they didn't talk to the host much. This creates a plethora of problems because not only does it lower the host's score, but it affects their visibility on the website, status and reputation… Hosts are outraged by how the reviews work and often contact us demanding that we fix this by adding a fifth star to a review, for example. We cannot do it, because it would be lying and manipulating stats. We have to let the host take the bullet. Their score has to be lowered, all because of a 4-star review that a guest left, thinking it would do the host some good.

Observing a host's reaction is like observing a chimpanzee in a laboratory. I'm studying their attitude, trying to understand their anger. It's all justified to me. These people want to do well, but our platform is designed to trick them. It's made so that they must pay fees for situations they can't control. They have to keep their reputation intact to get bookings. It's a lot of pressure; a single mistake can undo years of good behaviour and compliance. Getting ten '5 stars' reviews won't make up for a single '1-star'. It's unbalanced and conceived to service Blue's needs and policies. Failing to comply means it's the end of the host's business. Blue will be favouring another host and collect the fees of the previous one who failed them. It's a win-win situation for Blue. They created an environment of competition where hosts have to fall in line and have no room for rebellion. This is how it is, and that's the end of the story. To a certain extent, I believe hosts and agents are in a similar position. We're both being held on a leash and powerless against the corporation. The tricky schemes they're running do not give us any choice but to oblige, and contesting is pointless: we're all replaceable. And yet, without the agents, there's no support. The gears wouldn't be running without us. And they wouldn't without the hosts either. At what point did we allow Blue to have so much power over us for the work that we're providing? I cannot wrap my brain around it. The hosts can't either. They're letting us know about how they feel on a regular basis. They can talk freely, at least, unlike us. Sadly, they're lashing out at us. We can only listen and sympathise, but there's nothing else we can do for them. We cannot initiate any change. We can tell them that we will forward their feedback to Blue, though writing it on a piece of paper and throwing it in the bin would have the same effect.

'*We're in the same boat*', I wish I could say.

Alas, I'm contractually obligated to defend our abuser and to endure the frustration of another party who's been just as mistreated as I was.

Telling a customer that their call is recorded is crucial. It is a legal requirement, and I have failed to mention it a few times. I've been caught doing this twice, and I'm told that the third time will get me a strike on my record. From that moment onwards, and after a meeting with my manager that I wish I never had, I made sure to comply and never forgot to inform the customer. I even leave a sticky note on my computer screen to always be reminded. I received a quality evaluation a few weeks later. My score is 0%. It says I failed to inform the customer our call was being recorded. The evaluation was followed by a message from Doris; she said we needed to talk. I'm nervous, but I'm also surprised. I swore that I would be the perfect agent, and I know that I mention the recording of the call every single time. It happens to forget, of course, but I know this is not my case. I strongly believe that I'm being tricked here. I asked the quality evaluator to listen to the call another time, and she did. She came back to me and said that I did not mention that the call was being recorded and that my evaluation would not change. I met with my manager, and she started telling me about the strike. I object. I told her that I strongly believed the evaluator was mistaken, and I asked her to listen to the call. She refuses at first, but I decide to insist. I'm sure of myself, and I took enough abuse from this company to give them yet another chance to make fun of me. I ask for the recording of the call every day, and after a week of requesting it, my manager gets it. Doris asks me to come into a meeting with her. She plays the audio file. A few seconds pass, and I make small talk with the user. It's someone I previously had on the phone and had to call back. I guess I can say we knew each other enough to joke around and talk for a bit before getting into the actual resolution of the problem. And this is precisely what happened. The customer and I were chatting about their holiday and laughing for the first 30 seconds of the call. After that, I tell them that I'll be changing the topic to discuss the resolution of their case. Doris pauses the call.

'As you can hear, you failed to mention the call was being recorded', she says.

I'm not buying it. 'Please continue to play it,' I ask.

She does not want to. She takes a few seconds before pressing play again, exhaling loudly as if she was tired of it already. The call continues. I start explaining to the user what I'm doing for 10 seconds and then stop.

'Oh, before I forget...', I say, 'You already know, but this call is being recorded for training and quality purposes...'

'Yeah, I remember', he answers. 'You told me that the last time too, I still consent'.

Here it was. The proof was in the pudding. It took 40 seconds for me to realise that I did not fail to follow the company's guidelines after all. I was in the right, and yet Doris and the quality department did everything they could to make me believe otherwise. I jumped from my chair.

'Here! Did you hear?' I almost yell.

'Oh yeah...' she says.

I can tell she feels stupid. She hates being wrong, but she plays so much by the rules that she cannot deny the obvious. I will not be getting a strike. She has to remove it from my file as I watch after I request it. I do not trust her to do it on her own after that. She tells me that she will let the quality agent know and that we can forget about the strike, and I quote, 'For now.'

At this moment, something is shifting in me. This company created a hostile and stressful environment for me to work with, and now, it is obvious that it was also designed to make me fail. I accepted this job mostly because of the high salary it was offering. Bonuses were promised. I'm now convinced that none of these bonuses can be attributed to agents if such schemes are deployed to keep them away from our paychecks. I am being framed. It is fraud; it is not the truth, and it is wrong. The worst part is that I hesitated to speak up. I never do. I don't dare to go against Doris usually because she made it so that the team fears her. This time, I felt like it was enough. I have had enough from her and from the company. I can't sleep properly that night. I feel angry, and I have resentment inside me. I keep wondering if they did this on purpose or if they did not care to listen to more than 10 seconds of my call before evaluating me.

I'm not sure which one is worse. After all, these people are being paid to listen to my calls. I'm not kidding when I say they're some of the laziest employees around. In any case, I'm at my wit's end with the company. I can no longer bear my condition; I feel trapped and abused, and my mental health is getting worse each week. Seeing how Coralie got promoted also made me realise that the idea of progress in Blue isn't what I imagined. I won't be going to a better place, only a worse one. Whatever department they decide to move me to won't be my choice, and it will be even more draining. I wanted to do something fun, like HR or quality. There was never a talk about the possibility of ending up in either of these teams. It's always customer support on a different level of urgency. This is not the career path I was dreaming of, and if I don't act now, I won't have any sanity left to even dream. It's decided: I'm going to quit.

Chapter 4: Yellow

A colleague of mine, Lola, decides to quit Blue to apply for another job. She says the company 'Yellow' is looking for new 'advisors'. *I love the fancy names.* It takes a few days to sink in, but I'm finally intrigued by this position. The advertisement is still online, which means they're still recruiting. I try my luck. I'm rotting here in Blue, and I do not see the end of it. I need some change, and I need to save myself from this moving sand I'm slowly being sucked into. I prepared my resume and added my experience as a customer support agent for Blue at the top of the page. This makes my profile stand out, and I'm getting an interview a few days later.

The company Yellow is a leader in the gaming industry. As a big fan of video games, this sounds like the perfect job to me. Once again, I'm asked to name my favourite video games. I make sure to include titles that the company produces to perfect my ass-licking skills. The interviews go smoothly; I don't really feel like I'm being interviewed. We do some role-play, and they pretend to be a customer asking me difficult questions. I've been on the battlefront for months now; this does not scare me. I'm able to bounce off everything they throw at me with ease and make the recruiting process sound easy. They send me a contract and a starting date. I write a resignation letter for Blue via email. I am filled with joy and satisfaction as I click 'Send'. Doris tells me that she's devastated. She asks if we can keep in touch. I don't answer.

What I'm the most excited about is the change of contract. This time, the company Yellow will be hiring me directly. They're not outsourcing, which means I will be a Yellow employee. Great benefits come along, such as better pay, health insurance, and many company benefits which aren't negligible.

I start the training for Yellow two weeks later. They sent me a brand-new computer and other equipment. This is a change; everything they send is new and clean, and some of the latest products are on the market. This makes me feel like I'm worth something. I'm going to be dedicating 40 hours a week of my time to them, and it seems like they are grateful for it. On top of that, I received a welcoming box which included a hoodie, a tee shirt, a mug, a notebook, a beanie, some candies, and a lot more things I can't remember.

The training for Yellow will last one month. I'm being taught alongside four other colleagues of mine, which are all nice. I have several trainers who each have a specialty. Some are more customer-oriented, while others are more tech-savvy. They're all nice and engage a lot with me. The job requires me to play video games, and for the first month, I'm doing this. I feel like this is a dream come true. On afternoons, mostly, we're being asked to launch one specific game and to play it for 2 to 3 hours. And we're getting paid for it. This sounds awesome, and it makes sense that, as a support agent, I should know what I'm talking about. If a player contacts me about a game, I have to be able to answer their questions. This means I have to be playing the game to understand it. This is logical, but I never thought a company would really pay me to play video games. This is a sign that this job is better than the previous one and that my decision to switch was not going to be regretted.

We're being shown the exact systems which we will be using on the job and are being prepared for real-case scenarios. We are watching our colleagues work, and we study their ways. We're being given relevant information about our roles and the products we will support, and we are being introduced to different colleagues from different departments. This creates a nice working environment and motivates me to do a good job. This is the great side of the corporate world I've never seen. This is what companies wish they were, but this one actually was.

The people who are in my training are nice. I know my friend Lola, who was previously working in Blue with me. The new hires that are in our group are all kind as well. They have different backgrounds, and not all of them are gamers. They all have the right attitude, though. We connect quite fast as we're a much smaller group than we were during the training in Blue. I think Yellow favours quality over quantity. We are introduced to the senior agents who will be guiding us during our first weeks. I'm also getting to know my manager, Damiano. I'm not done with my training yet, and I already have a manager. He's completely different from the terrible Doris. He's nice and funny and never mentions any metrics. Whenever we talk, we talk about me: my aspirations, my feelings. I went from sour to sweet.

One of the senior agents who's been assigned to my group to help us is called Freya. She's a bit older than me, and she is the most nonchalant girl I've ever met. Our manager has set up a conference call on which she must be present during the whole day. Whenever a new hire like me needs help, we can jump on a call and ask for her assistance. This is a tedious and demanding task. Freya does not hesitate to let us know how she feels about it. I jumped on the call one day.

'Freya, I have a quick question…' I ask, super shy.

—' Oh my fucking g … WHAT AGAIN?!' She shouts.

Call me a masochist, but I liked it when she did that. I don't like to be shouted at, of course. But at least I know that she speaks from the heart, and she's a straight shooter. Her authenticity clashes with the fakeness I had to put up with In Blue. This is the first time in a company that I've met an honest person. I laugh. She helps me with my case for 10 minutes before she asks:

'All good now? Can I go back to playing my game, or are you going to bust my nuts again?'

She was playing a video game. And I dared to interrupt. As a gamer myself, I know this is grounds for murder. I got assistance from her, and she got my respect.

My training is slowly coming to an end. At the end of the week, all the other trainees and I play games together. We exchange phone numbers, and we regularly text. The job is starting at a much better pace than any other before. I'm well prepared to face any type of interaction. After months in hell, this feels like a walk in the park. There are a lot of similarities in the way we document cases and greet customers. The administrative part of the job remains more or less the same. The customers are different because they're gamers, so they're a lot more chill. Some of them are technical experts and want precise troubleshooting. Others are more tempered and call to complain about losing their game. I get parents on the phone whose kids stole their credit cards to spend money on a game. I also get kids asking if they can get games for free since they don't have a credit card to steal at the moment. Overall, the issues are a lot lighter than in Blue. It's making me chuckle most of the time. When I meet with Lola, who brought me to Yellow, we don't discuss the job that much. We mention it, but we don't obsess over it like we used to with Blue. I still get in touch with my former colleagues who are still working there. The only topic on their mind is Blue. They need to talk about it. Now that I'm free from this prison, I have an outside view of what Blue employees look like. It's not a pretty sight. I wonder if anyone thought the same about me during my time as their employee. I certainly can tell now. I'm more radiant.

Quite frankly, I have no complaints about this job so far. I'm enjoying it. My colleagues are nice, the company offers great benefits, and the job itself is good enough. It's not too repetitive; the customers aren't rude for now. I also get to play video games most of the time, so there's little to no downside here. Yellow also has a unique way of encouraging teamwork, which is one of the best initiatives I've seen. Each agent gets a certain amount of points every month that they can give away to their colleagues as a thank-you gift for their help on a case or a project. The agent receiving the points will be able to spend them in the company's shop, which offers gift cards and other goodies. The points given are different from the points received, meaning that agents can't give themselves points or use the balance which is meant to be sent to the shop. This encourages cooperation and rewards each employee for their actions, no matter how small. Unlike Blue, Yellow offers financial compensation for remote workers to help with the cost of electricity and broadband. They also offer free video games for employees, as well as for our friends and family. Joining Yellow after months of torture in Blue feels like I just escaped a concentration camp and found shelter in Willy Wonka's chocolate factory.

Freya and I are growing closer. We find out that we have similar tastes in video games, music, and movies. We send each other memes, and she helps me install new games on my working computer. I can't be thankful enough for Yellow to be allowing this. There's a game that I've always wanted to play on the PC, but I never had a powerful enough one of my own to try it out. Yellow's equipment is some of the best I've ever seen. I bet we could run 4 video games at once on it. I buy and download the game. I started to play it for a little bit. Experiencing joy while working is a new feeling for me. If I were to Google something out of the ordinary on Blue's computer, I would get a strike. In Yellow, I'm given the freedom and trust to do whatever I want on my PC. I feel on top of the world.

The next morning, I turned on my computer, and it instantly crashed. I'm curious; this has never happened before. I tried to restart it again, but the same thing happened. I wonder what could've caused this. The only thing I did differently the day before was installing that new game. Perhaps I messed up a driver or deleted an important source file. The computer simply won't start. I'm getting anxious, and my stomach feels heavy. I haven't been feeling like this in a while. I believe I will be getting in trouble. I message my manager, and he laughs when I tell him. He reassures me and says that I shouldn't worry. He does not seem concerned. He does what's necessary, and I received a new computer 3 days later. The person delivering the new computer also picked up the old one that I had just destroyed with my game.

The more I get calls and emails, the more I get to know Yellow's customers. I know what they want, how they like to be talked to, and what games they prefer to play. In this job, I come across the most fascinating person I've ever seen. Tim and I don't know more about him than this; he emails and initiates chats with us several times a day. I'd say, on average, he contacts us 10 times a day, but it can go up to 30 if he is in good shape. The reason why he contacts us is the same all the time, 'Why did your company steal games I own?'. It comes in several variations. Sometimes, it is all in cap, sometimes with 3 exclamation points at the end of its sentence. This makes me believe he manually types in every message he is sending, not simply copy-pasting them. Tim is a myth in himself. A legend in the team. Our department has its own mythology, and Tim is the Zeus the Greeks would be jealous of. He is our reason to get up in the morning. The mystery behind this man is that no one actually knows what he's talking about. We are told not to engage and to close each interaction we have with him. I asked my manager why this man insisted on contacting us every day. He told me that a few years ago, Tim was banned from our services, which made it impossible for him to join our platform and play our free games. Tim does not own any paid games. He was solely playing the free games. He would probably have a case for himself if he actually bought something that he would want to claim back, but apparently, all that he was after was the save of our main free game that he lost several years ago. I don't know what he achieved in the game for him to be asking for it back so fiercely, but I am fascinated every time he pops up on my screen. The sensation I feel every time I receive a chat notification accusing me of stealing his property makes me shiver. I try to ask questions to get to the bottom of it. 'Can you explain the situation to me, please?' I ask.

—' You stole from me! YOU THIEF'. He writes back.

There is no talking to this guy. We're better off blocking him. This is an option we have. But Tim, as loyal as he is, creates new email addresses every time we ban one of his accounts for harassment. And we're talking about a guy who contacts us every hour or so. We're probably blocking 50 email addresses each week, only for him to create new ones with even more creative names. Sometimes, it's just a series of numbers with the domain name at the end. Sometimes, he finds himself a new username to try out for the week. It's like watching Odysseus coming back to Ithaca all over again. The man is dedicated to the task like no one I've ever seen. I'm amazed by the amount of time he's ready to spend each day just getting blocked as soon as he types in one message. Tim is using several email providers to create new addresses that he can use to contact us. Creating an email address requires verifying captchas, those images where we have to select all the bikes to prove that we're not robots. He also has to fill out a form to get in touch with us. Doing this would probably take between 5 to 10 minutes for one interaction. He does this several times every single day. I wouldn't have believed it if I didn't witness it with my own eyes. Insanity in its purest form. From the day I started going to live until now, he has been here. I respect this man's commitment and want to honour him as the single most disturbed person I've ever come across.

It's Lola who brought me to Yellow. She left Blue only a few months after she started the job because she instantly felt like it was going to ruin her mentally. She is very insightful. She seems to be sensing that something is off with Yellow, too. One day, she mentioned it to me. She tells me that she's going to quit and that she no longer wants to work here. She says she doesn't like the job and has some growing concerns about the company. I really can't see it personally. I'm in my honeymoon phase, and nothing can't disturb me for now. But seeing Lola leave makes a big change in my environment. The dynamic isn't the same without her in the team, and I no longer have someone to fully confide in. I'm sad, but I'm used to people quitting, so I get it. Customer support isn't for everyone, and Lola has never really been a gamer. It didn't work for her, but it will for me, I'm sure of it.

During our weekly team meeting, she announces her departure. We all wish her well, and we tell her that we'll miss her.

A few weeks later, on our team group chat, we received a message from Damiano. He tells us that he hired a new person to replace Lola. It's a French girl, and she's going to start work the next week. Because she's in training right now, she joined our group chat so that one of our teammates could help her the same way I was helped when I started. Upon joining the group, we discovered her face through the profile picture she uploaded on our messaging system. Her name is Kylie, and she has beautiful green eyes. She looks like a Disney princess, so charming and elegant. I hear a notification sound. It's a message from Freya. She sent me an emoji with a heart in its eyes. I think she's falling in love with the new hire.

'I think I'm falling in love!' She messaged me 2 minutes later.

Girl, I guessed. She sends the following message to Kylie:

'Hello Kylie! : -) Welcome to Yellow!!! If you need help with anything, please don't hesitate to reach out to me personally; I will be happy to help. Really, anything at all, don't be shy: -). Are you finding everything OK? If you're lost and need to go over something from the training, let me know! (several heart emojis)'.

I'm dying when I see this. I'm not used to seeing Freya bend over backwards for someone. I never thought she would be using heart emojis one day. I thought she didn't know they existed. Kylie feels the warm welcome and thanks us for our kindness. We do our best to include her in the team and provide her with all the necessary guidance to make sure she can succeed. The teamwork in Yellow is our strongest suit.

I quickly get along with Kylie. We have many things in common. I offer my help in some cases, but she says that Freya is already watching over her like a guardian angel in the sky. I don't want to step on Freya's toes; I'm scared she will retaliate by setting me on fire.

Lola's departure remains a bit of a shock for me. I can't wrap my head around what could've pushed her to leave a job that I find so perfect. I try to keep my eyes open to understand her point of view. I don't want to become my own self-fulfilled prophecy. And yet, after a while, I start to notice. Somewhere in the shadow, something was lurking and waiting for the right moment to strike. As usual, a routine begins, and I start to focus more on the company and its decline. The first one is because of the quality department. In Yellow, the agents meticulously follow their quality guidelines and commit little to no mistakes. For quality agents, this is a good and bad thing at the same time. It is good because it means the quality standards they set can be met and that agents understand them well enough to follow them. It is bad because now they have nothing else to do. Reviewing customer interaction does not take long. They probably review one or two interactions per agent each week. Interactions are commonly 10 minutes long, making the evaluation process relatively short. These people have 40 hours a week to kill. If I'm being nice, I'd say they can do all their evaluations within a day for all the agents they were assigned. What about the four other days they have until the weekend? In Yellow, they decided to use this time by changing their guidelines, updating their process, and essentially making the agents work harder. '*If it ain't broke, you don't need to fix it*', we say. This is not their mantra at all. Each week, quality agents would find creative ways to change up our way of working because of a recent revelation that they had. They suddenly want us to use bullet points in our notes, or they want us to give our names at the beginning of the call. It started slowly before becoming unbearable. 'Empathy', they said. 'You have to show empathy'. Apparently, when a user is having a difficult time or when we can't process their request, we aren't being empathetic enough. Quality agents, after 3 weeks of brainstorming, came up with a genius new plan to interact with our customers. We are no longer allowed to say 'sorry' because it has a negative connotation. We should say that we understand their point of view, that the situation is frustrating and that we feel for them. We're given phrases to recite for these situations, and it completely clashes with the rest of the call. Yellow always gave us the liberty to talk to the customers in our preferred way, allowing us to be authentic and relaxed and to create genuine interaction. Now, we are given these phrases to place in our calls; it's weird. The people can tell that it is not coming from us. *'I understand this is frustrating'*. Who talks like that? Certainly not me. I can feel a shift from that moment onwards. Customers are not as nice anymore. Because the moment we start with our pre-written speech, they immediately go into defense mode. They're convinced that they're talking to a robot and will not use the human language of seeking help, but will rather use the more pressing verbiage of demanding something. As soon as they feel like there's no talking to us, they raise their voices and order us to process their request. The change is notable, and I'm not as comfortable as I used to be when answering a phone call. All because quality agents deemed that it was mandatory to deliver these sympathy statements, which they probably learned somewhere under a yurt in a Gwyneth Paltrow seminar.

The team cohesion is a lot better in Yellow than it was in Blue. This is a gaming company, so the profile of the employees is generally more chill than usual. We can send each other memes in our group chat. We can share music videos and funny anecdotes. We also help each other in a funny way.

'What can I recommend to a customer who has an error 102 when trying to start their game?' I ask.

—' You can tell them to go fuck themselves', Freya advises.

Even Damiano laughs. The vibe is totally different. It's like night and day. Another colleague who knows the error 102 sent me an explanation of the problem, why it is happening and how to fix it. He even sent me a pre-written message that I could directly send to the user to solve my case. This is teamwork at its finest. My colleagues all have different tastes in video games. Some of them prefer horror games, while others prefer construction games. Nonetheless, they're all eager to play. They set up gaming nights and invited me to join after work. I accept and I try out new games I never played before. Because they're Yellow games, I can play them for free. This is such an enjoyable experience. I get to know my team on a more personal level, and I get to play video games for free. This is the absolute dream. This is what I wished Purple was. It took me years before I could finally enjoy work, but I got there.

My team gets along so well that we decide to meet up in Dublin for the weekend. Our schedule at Yellow isn't far-fetched. We do regular office hours, Monday to Friday. This is a luxury in itself because we're free every weekend, and our bodies have a routine they can get used to. I met all of my team, and I'm once again experiencing this weird feeling of recognising someone's voice but not their face. It takes me a while to acknowledge that I know the person in front of me; I have never met them in person before. Freya arrives last. She walks in with Kylie. I greet them, and I learn that they came together by car because they had just moved in together. I look at Freya.

'She needed a place to stay, so I told her we could become housemates'. Freya tries to justify herself the best she can.

I give her a look. She gives me a look. We understood each other. Well played, my dear.

We spend the night drinking in a healthy manner, not obsessing over our job. Instead, we talk about our lives and what we were doing before moving to Ireland, for example. It's a different kind of night than the one I'm used to. These people are my colleagues, but we behave like friends. We have several topics of conversation, and we don't sound like broken records. We discuss politics, and nothing goes awry. This is a testament to how open-minded we all are. Kylie and Freya tell us they have to leave because they have a long drive ahead of them. I smile. We call it a night, and all go home.

The party ends, and I notice that my alcohol consumption is lower than before. I'm proud of myself.

The trainers who took care of me during my first weeks regularly checked on me to see how I had improved. The meetings I have with them are really pleasant; they're always smiling and making jokes. I meet them once a month, and each time, they tell me that I will have to improve my statistics. I need to make more calls, solve more cases, and get better customer satisfaction. It starts slowly, but it becomes quite demanding after some time. As the expectations get higher, the tone shifts. There's no honey in their voice anymore, and the request feels more like an order. New agents have been hired, and we jump on a meeting to greet them. I noticed that the trainers addressed the new agents the same way they used to address me, with a lot of sweetness. I remark how they're no longer nice to me, and I wonder if this was a strategy all along. I'm traumatised by the way I was treated in Blue. I can't help but feel like I was tricked once again into believing that this job isn't what it is. The main focus is obviously the numbers, as it always was. I have to be realistic about this. I wonder if this is what Lola thought, too.

Though Yellow has a lot of pros, I can't say that it does not have any cons. The downsides of this job are mostly felt by us women, who have a harder time than men in this specific role. The video game industry is sexist, and most of our customers are men. When a female agent is picking up a male customer's call, that man will automatically believe that he's talking to an imbecile and will not be afraid to say so. Men and women are treated alike in the workplace. We receive the same training and have access to the same resources. Some of my female colleagues are actually super keen on sports and combat games, which are considered more 'manly' games. They would provide better support for these games than some other male colleagues. This is a hard pill for Yellow's customers to swallow. A lot of the time, when a man asks for assistance on a game they play all day, they cannot conceive that a woman would be helpful. They're rejecting any support, claiming that they're 'just a girl and can't possibly know what they're talking about'. As a result, all my female colleagues and I are changing our agent support's name to a man's name so that when a customer is initiating a chat, they will be talking to a man. Unfortunately, this trick can't work over the phone, and we are doomed to have to deal with this farce on a daily basis. We have instances of customers calling back until they can get a man on a line. The male agents will provide the exact same answers as a female agent, but for some reason, this time, because it's been voiced a few octaves lower, the resolution is accepted. This happens with customers playing specific games, seen as 'men's games'.

As if this wasn't enough for us, the women in Yellow also have to deal with another type of customer: the ones who are falling in love over the phone. Unlike their sexist playmates, some male customers think having a woman on the line is the greatest thing ever because it means that a woman who has knowledge of video games is actively talking to them. A woman playing video games is enough to blow the minds of many male players, teenagers and adults alike. They switch their voice to honey mode, make terrible jokes, and finally ask for the agent's phone number or social media contacts. Because it is expected of us to remain professional and friendly, we have no choice but to fake laughter, pretend to be flattered and politely decline the invitation to become friends. It takes a few no's to terminate the call. Sometimes, customers come back and ask for the call to be transferred to a specific female agent because their last call, which lasted 4 minutes, sure created a hell of a bond. This happens a lot in Yellow, but this scenario isn't specific to this company. Women in customer support will often find themselves facing male clients asking for their phone number or to go on a date. It's baffling to me that in such a setting, someone would have the nerve to ask for an agent's phone number. Any agent, male or female, is supposed to be nice on the phone. This isn't a flirting tactic; this is a work requirement which is heavily monitored and severely punished if not applied. Failing to understand this is perplexing to me, but not everyone has been blessed with the gift of intelligence at birth. This is, unfortunately, a curse for all my female coworkers and myself, who don't even have the strength to complain about it anymore.

Because support has to operate in many languages, most agents are not Irish. In fact, almost none of them are.

Agents are coming from abroad, from Portugal, Italy, France ... to provide customer support in their mother tongue while working in English. More often than not, the agents moved out of their country specifically for this job and have no family in Ireland. This means that every once in a while, they wish to go back to their hometown to spend time with their family for birthdays, Christmas or weddings. This does bring up an important point, which is that agents only have 25 vacation days a year. This is pretty standard. But if most of these vacation days are being used to see our family in our hometown, we don't really have much left to go on an actual holiday. This happens across all support companies, and a tendency is starting to appear: the need to work from abroad. Some companies are taking the lead and letting their employees work up to 2 weeks from abroad. Others are offering a whole month. I say 'offering' as if I'm talking about a gift from the heavens that the company is willing to give. In the corporate eyes, this is exactly it. Companies treat this benefit as a luxury that can only be granted on specific conditions that they set, and they reserve the right to refuse it to anyone who asks. There are no legal requirements obligating the company to offer a work-from-abroad scheme, but most employees simply do it on the employer's back. Combined with the fact that most agents are asking for it, that everyone is currently working from home, and that some companies are implementing it, Yellow has no choice but to surrender. However, they do their absolute best to fight back and not let the work-from-abroad be a thing. When we ask why, they say it's because it will bring a lot of tax-related complications. When we ask which ones, they stop answering. As far as I know, most complications would be on the employee's end, having to pay taxes in 2 countries if they are to stay too long working in a different country. The employer can be liable for some taxes, but the conditions are so broad and situational that I don't think any company ever had to face this situation, let alone pay any taxes for an employee who works from abroad. This is a small win for us agents, who are getting rid of our paid time off at the speed of light for mental health reasons already. We now have a chance to potentially enjoy a full week of holiday. Of course, the latter has to be approved, which is often not the case. We all want to go during the summer, for example, and there can only be so many of us away at the same time. As a result, we're often asked to take holidays in random periods just to align with everyone else's schedule. Since we can't carry vacation days from one year to the next, we have to rest when we're told, not when we decide.

We learn about the release of an upcoming game. Damiano informed us that we would receive a lot of chats, emails, and calls the following week. I prepare myself accordingly. I save in my notes some pre-written messages that I can copy and paste for certain situations. That way, I can deal with my cases faster. I can receive 3 chats at once, so I'd better be ready. The moment we've all been waiting for finally arrives. The game is out, and all hell breaks loose. The phone lines are saturated. There are more than 50 calls waiting to be connected to an agent. I receive many chats. Once I close one, another one starts. This is unlike anything we've ever seen. Damiano prepared us for this, and encourages us regularly. He even partakes in the job. He takes some calls and answers emails. This is astonishing. Damiano knows how to work our job. He knows what he's talking about, and he's willing to help in times of need. This contrasts with Doris, who threw rocks at us from her ice tower when we weren't writing emails fast enough. Damiano is pushing us to do well and helping us make the effort. I respect the hell out of him for that. This also means that there's a before and after the customer support position. If he knows how to answer emails, it's because he's done it in the past. And now he's a manager. He evolved professionally and climbed the corporate ladder to secure a better position for himself. Maybe this isn't a myth after all. I regain hope that one day, I'll be able to do the same. For now, though, I need to take calls. There are 50 people waiting for me to help them.

The insane amount of calls and chats exhaust me. I can usually take it easy during certain days, but this is no longer the case. This new game release saturated our lines, and we don't have a minute of rest. My colleagues asked if I wanted to join tonight's game. I decline the invitation. I'm too tired to stay a minute more on my office chair. I can't even focus on the computer screen anymore. I jump in bed, and I fall asleep immediately at 5 p.m. I feel like I just worked a day in a hospital after a natural disaster.

Weeks pass, and I get a glimpse of the full scope of user issues. I started with simple troubleshooting, but now I'm getting all of the colours of the rainbow. This new game release also drastically increased the number of contacts we receive every day and, consequently, the number of unpleasant calls with it.

Yellow is best known for one particular game, in which it is possible to make some in-game purchases. After purchasing the game, players can make additional purchases within the game for some additional gear, unlock some characters or customise the latter. One purchasing option is notoriously controversial, as it offers a random reward for a set price. The reward can be common or rare, depending on luck, rare rewards being obviously obtained only a small percentage of the time. Whether these rewards are given randomly or not, I cannot say. It does not matter that much to me. I only have to deal with customers who are unhappy with their purchase, of course, so I only know of people who got the wrong end of the stick. It only occurred once that a customer called to say they actually got a rare loot and wanted to thank me personally for it. Because of the lack of recognition I got from my company, I told them, 'You're welcome'. Most of the users, however, are unhappy with their purchase. It's explicitly stated that they can get a common reward, which is worth less than the random purchase option, but it does not make it less frustrating for the person buying it. The in-game transactions are non-refundable, so it leaves room for support to be the target of user complaints. I'm thorned on the topic.

It's difficult for me to pity grown adults who willingly put their hard-earned money in an in-game lottery, and yet, I can't help but feel like this is a pure exploitation of a human vice, just like cigarettes and alcohol. It's gambling. Some countries treat this functionality as such and have banned it altogether. Others regulate it more. Unfortunately, the majority of countries do not have any laws in place to fight or prevent this form of addiction, and I'm not even sure that they're aware of it. Some groups have been formed to defend consumer rights, but this remains insufficient. Our terms of service are clear: no refunds will be provided. The company knows that the players will keep on spending money on their game and will continue to do so. The support department is the only one the players can reach out to for their complaints, and they aren't given the tools to refund anything. That's a perfect scheme to unethically gross money without having to be confronted with the damages it does. Customers are not happy about it and want their voices to be heard, which is understandable. In an unfortunate series of events, it happens that the person who's been hired to listen to people's complaints is me. I'm forced by a contract to answer calls from users who are not happy about a purchase they made willingly, demanding a refund I cannot grant. It's sort of like driving a one-way street, and a car is facing mine, but none of us move to let the other pass. It can last hours; there's no resolution possible here. I notice that some customers are affected more than others. Some of them are confessing that they spent their entire salary on the game and don't know how they'll afford their children's food. I'm at a loss for words when I hear this. These people are idiots, sick, or both. I feel sorry and angry that this is the situation I have to deal with on a regular. Other phone calls are equally unpleasant. Unhappy customers threaten to kill me, rape me or behead me. I would take it with humour if I didn't know that some of them could actually track me down because of how unemployed they are. The worst one was a dad calling me and saying unspeakable things he would do to me as a woman. It broke my heart to hear his daughter's voice in the back, realising this person is a parent. I can report them to my manager for an outstanding 2-week ban from the game, essentially meaning that I'm releasing a monster from its cage for 2 weeks so it can touch some grass. The company does not take these threats seriously and won't until something tragic happens one day. They don't retaliate when someone threatens an employee of rape and murder because of policies they put in place. The only time they moved a finger was when someone expressed their interest in placing a bomb in our office. I suspect they went the extra mile after the same user confirmed the exact location of the office. Another joy of a customer to have is the one who says they're going to end their lives if they don't get what they want. This happens more often than anyone would wish, and we're unable to do anything in this situation as well. We're being told to end the call as we're not meant to deal with this situation. After all, we're not therapists, nor are we trained on the topic at all. And it's true, we are not. Yellow acknowledges that the support agents are not trained to deal with suicidal customers but expresses no remorse for the gambling addicts they take advantage of every day. The company only wants us to deal with one kind of mental sickness, the one they can capitalise on.

Receiving rape wishes and suicide calls starts to have an effect on me and my well-being. Though it's not the majority of the calls I get in a day, they're definitely the ones that stick with me. Yellow does not offer psychological help or mental rest; they expect me to shrug it off. They know that this is what I have to deal with, and they know it's hard. Regardless, it's not important for them. As long as I keep the unhappy customers away from them, they're free to enjoy their golf afternoon.

Some customers are aware that I'm not the person responsible for their unhappiness.

'It's not against you,' they say after calling me names for 10 minutes.

This is usually the moment where I should be reassured. This man wasn't threatening me personally; he was threatening the company I'm working for. Though I can understand this type of comment, it doesn't change the fact that I'm the one who has to listen to a series of complaints every day. Complaints I'm not responsible for, and cannot make better in any way. People need someone to complain to; they need to let out their frustration and anger. In a way, the support phone number is also a complaint hotline. Users know they won't get a resolution but will feel better after 30 minutes of virtually punching an agent who cannot retaliate at all. But it's not against me. That makes it immediately OK now to be physically threatened and mentally tortured every day. Again, this is not the majority of the calls, but one call of the sort is enough to overshadow 40 nice ones, making me forget about all the good sides of humanity, only to remember horrid words.

After another week of dealing with the aftermath of that game release, my team asked if I'd be joining the video game night after my shift. I refuse. I can't stay a minute more in front of a computer. I feel the need to breathe some fresh air and feel the sunlight on my face. I live in Dublin, of course, so I won't get any of these. But at least I go out of my room, and I'm no longer forced to receive these calls.

I need my monthly dose of complaining about work, and I need to get out of my house. I asked my colleagues if they wanted to meet up with me again this weekend, and they said yes. We set up a pub night. Freya and Kylie arrive last, again. This time, they're holding hands.

'We're taking things slow, says Kylie with a smirk.

I give her a look. She gives me a look. We understood each other. Well played, my dear.

One of my colleagues, Joanna, is missing. We tried to call her, but she didn't answer. I learned that it's been weeks since she did not leave the house. She developed a form of anxiety so severe she could no longer go out. We think it's because of the amount of calls we receive every day. It's a lot. It's more than the average person would take in a year. It's an industrial level of support that we have to provide, and what we receive in return is not always pleasant. I can see how that affects her. I go to the pub and order one pint. When I go back to my table, I start complaining about the job. The team follows my lead. I complain about the customers, the lack of support from the company, and how the trainers are no longer nice to me. We all agree that something has shifted. I remember now that Lola saw it coming. She tried to warn me. I didn't believe her like the Trojans didn't believe Cassandra when she told them there were men hidden in that horse. Here I am now. Drowning my sorrow once again at the pub. I empty pints after pints. It's starting again. I've been working in Yellow for as long as I've been working in Blue. Maybe this is my breaking point. Maybe I can't do customer support for longer than this. I strongly believed that Yellow was different, but here I am. I'm still receiving abuse on a daily basis and complaining about it with my colleagues at the pub. I notice the demeanour on our faces, too. It has changed since the last time we met. I think we all know that the honeymoon phase is over. We're being struck with the reality of the job. After all, this is customer support. It's not meant to be a vocation.

I need to evolve professionally. I need to do it quickly before I become insane again. The barman comes and tells us that the pub will close soon. I think I could've drunk a couple more pints. Some colleagues offer to continue drinking at home. I'm not sure I reached that level of desperation yet. I wait to see everyone else's answer to this offer. Freya and Kylie decline. They say they need to leave because they have a long night ahead of them. I smile. I go home, too. I turned off my phone so as not to see my bank notifications about how much I had spent on drinks that night.

After a few months, I notice that I'm becoming an old hag. And not a cool hag like Freya. A grumpy one like Doris. Because of how unimportant the video games issues are, it's difficult for me to be invested in the resolution of certain problems. If a reward hasn't been granted to a player after completing a level like it should've: I don't see the urgency in the situation, despite the player I have over the phone having a panic attack. There's nothing at stake, and since there were no payments involved, I'm simply not concerned. The issues in Blue felt more real, and the stress they induced followed me all day. This contrasts drastically with the issues I'm facing in Yellow. I sometimes let out a laugh when a customer explains their issue to me. I can't take them too seriously. I also can't really fix anything here. I'm not a coder, and I can't get one involved anyway. It's just bad luck and we'll have to call it a day. It's hard news to deliver a player so passionate about a game, but it's the reality. I have no tools or resources at my disposal to fix these minor incidents. My best weapons, in this case, are my sharp hypnosis skills, also known as offering empathy to a user. With a bit of luck, they'll get over their banana badge not appearing in their inventory and will leave me alone.

This sounds like I'm not interested in helping customers. This is not the case at all. I would help anyone, no matter how important their issue is. Yellow has many games in their catalogue, some of them older than others. We have tools to provide support on the most recent ones and the most profitable ones. If the game is old or doesn't bring in any money, we won't have any tooling to fix any situation. We have to resort to troubleshooting we find on forums provided by the players themselves, who know the game better than us. It's very obvious to us that Yellow makes games for money only and not to provide an enjoyable gaming experience to their players. For this reason, our hands are tied when we are asked for help with certain titles. As much as I would like to help, I'm not equipped. I can provide virtual CPR such as 'restart your console', hoping for a miracle to happen, but if the game's heartbeat doesn't come back, then I won't be of any help.

To be honest, I'm just reaching a point of exhaustion. Replying to emails and calls gets really old. I've been doing this for so long it feels robotic. I feel like a robot. That's why support agents have the reputation to be cold and emotionless. Some of us really are. I feel like I am. What happened to my American dream of becoming the head of

HR? I need to set some things in motion. I want what Damiano has. Or a trainer position. Or a quality position, since all they seem to be doing is getting high and come up with stupid plans. I'm tired of being at the bottom of the ladder still. I feel like I suffered enough and I need all my hard work to be rewarded. I will act in consequence, and I will put myself out there to change my life for the better.

I spend weeks meeting with trainers and managers, sending them messages and emails. I join groups of colleagues who aren't from my team just so that they notice that I exist. I start to create some projects, I assist people with their own ongoing projects, and I try to make the most out of my situation. I feel like this is a wall I have to climb, and I'm ready for the challenge.

The last thing keeping me sane in Yellow is definitely my team. If it weren't for them, I think I would've left a long time ago. We're all still close, and I feel like I can count on them just like they can count on me. It's also nice to have deeper relationships than just colleagues.

Speaking of, on the weekend, I received a video from Freya. It's not a fight scene from Xena the Warrior, which is what she usually sends. I'm curious. It's a video of her riding a horse. How unusual for her. Kylie is beside her. I get it now. After a few minutes riding the horse, they both stop. Kylie reaches her pocket and takes out a little box. She opens it to reveal a gorgeous ring. I see Freya smiling with tears in her eyes. I'm still not used to it. My heart melts.

Freya gives her a look. Kylie gives her a look. They understood each other. Well played, my dears.

I have an ongoing issue with Yellow. The company has an obsession with working from home. At this time, there's a global pandemic, and the government guidelines do not allow offices to gather many employees in a closed space. Yellow insists that as soon as possible, they will require all employees to go back to the office. That is convenient, especially considering they hired a few people across the country who do not live in the office's city. Every 3 months or so, they're holding a meeting with employees all over the globe and they praise the work environment of an office. They say they miss it, and they would give anything to go back to it. I'm not sure if this is a meeting or an acting class on the theme 'Exaggeration'. Maybe I didn't get the memo. I'm also noticing a shift with some of my colleagues who are older than me and genuinely want to go back to an office to work. I have a hard time processing that information. I don't understand why we would need to wake up two hours in advance and spend an hour on public transport, all so that we could be sitting next to each other, not talking and being stuck in traffic on the way back home. I'm currently waking up 30 minutes before my shift starts, and I'm already home as soon as it ends. I'm happy with this. And I'm not the only one. Some colleagues are speaking up about the work from home situation and their wish to keep their current working situation intact. They make great points when they say that our stats are just as good, if not better when working from home and that employees are satisfied overall with their current workplace. Yellow refuses to change its mind, but after much pushback from employees, it decides to make a poll and ask who wants to stay at home and who wants to go back to the office. There's a third option which is to mix both, the 'hybrid' solution. The real results of this poll are never revealed, just like a Venezuelan's election results, and Yellow makes a final statement: we will all be back in the office as soon as the sanitary measures allow it.

Because of the pressuring demand, employees are slowly but surely commuting towards Dublin where the main office is located. This includes employees who were hired to work from home and are from other cities and sometimes countries. When advertising for the job, Yellow hired people from abroad before the lockdown was put in place. For months, and, in certain cases, years, these employees were contracted and worked for Yellow from abroad and were paid an Irish salary. This is because they signed their contract before the lockdown happened, making it impossible for them to go to Ireland. I guess working from abroad with an Irish contract isn't that hard after all. The pandemic is becoming an old memory, and everyone is now in Dublin. The employees moved, alone or with their family, they paid a deposit, bought a car, everything to start a new office life like Yellow asked. As a thank you gift for all the commitment, Yellow hosts a meeting with all the support agents. It's a bit unusual, but there shouldn't be a reason to get worried. After all they're not going to make us come all the way here only to fire us, right?

…

… Right?

Turns out that is exactly what they did. After months of pressuring their employees to have them come to Dublin, Yellow decided to fire all of the support department to relocate it in Budapest and India, where the workforce is considerably cheaper.

This feels like a slap in the face. It's so violent and sudden. All my dreams of making it in Yellow are dissolving into thin air. This is it. The end of this chapter. I really thought Yellow could be the one. The one company to change the trajectory of my professional career. Although the job became a lot heavier than it was at first, I still think I could've pulled through to make my way to the top. Damiano did it, and I believe that I could have done it, too. The floor is collapsing beneath my feet. All my plans and dreams are crushed because Yellow's executives want to save a few thousand euros each month. The support my team provide is excellent. The customers are satisfied. This company makes millions in profit every year, but this is not enough for them. They're going to sacrifice the quality of their customer support to increase the profit they can make. I'd like to say I'm surprised, but I'm not. I have a clear understanding of how corporations work nowadays. All of those who drastically changed their lives for this job have to go back to their home country without any savings because they put all of their money into the move. Some of my colleagues have to go back to living with their parents. Most of the agents will go back to their home country. It was a nice job for me. For many, it was more than that. Freya for example, could've done this forever. I can't help but feel sympathy for her. Since both she and Kylie are working for Yellow, it means they're now both unemployed, only a few weeks after getting engaged. This is the worst timing possible. We all feel defeated, angry, disappointed. My goal to become a corporate plant won't be achieved so soon. I have to face the hardships of a lay-off, and I now have to find another company to let me down.

Chapter 5: Grey

Leaving Yellow on such a bad note destroyed all my corporate hopes. I didn't think it would be possible for a customer support agent to lose their job because they cost too much money. We're probably one of the lowest-paid jobs in the country. We should be the ones leaving out of exhaustion, not the other way around. I feel like I just got dumped by someone who said, 'I can do better'. I don't have much time before I need to react. Those pints are expensive, and the cost of living in Ireland gets higher every day. I need a job, and I need one soon.

I apply for a handful of customer support jobs with the same objective in mind. I also try to be realistic: it could take time to find the right company for me. I will probably have to go through some questionable ones before I can go back on track in a nice environment.

The first company to get a hold of me is called Grey. It's an outsourcer which handles the support for clothing brands. They want me to become one of their agents for a specific brand that makes shoes and clothes. The salary they're offering is the lowest I've ever been offered. I think it's barely the legal minimum. I also checked the company reviews of previous employees who worked here; they all advised to stay away from Grey. I don't have the luxury of being picky, unfortunately. I have to accept as my time and money run out. I sign the contract, knowing full well that this time, I'm heading towards a disaster.

I recognise all the signs of a terrible company: a dirty and used computer shipped in a reused box with many torn stickers. I plug it in and set it up. I'm ready to go through this again.

This training is quite enjoyable, actually. I am joined by two other new hires who are both Italians. We get acquainted before meeting our trainer.

The man training us, Uri, is a nice 50-year-old man who is always smiling and happy to be on the call with us. He reminds me of these nice grandpas I would see in a park buying ice creams for their grandchildren despite the parents not wanting them to eat one before dinner. He has recurring jokes, meaning that he makes the same jokes every day. I'm not sure if he's aware or if he's been working here for so long that he can't tell what's coming out of his mouth. He tells the other recruits and myself that he's been in the company for 30 years. This shatters me. This man has been doing customer support for 30 years? I didn't know they even had customer support in the '90s. I thought we had just invented it. I'm also sad. Some part of me can't help but think that this poor guy has been doing the same robotic job for three decades now, and I'm saddened by his lack of perspective. Really, if he likes doing that, it's fine. I'm simply projecting myself that if I'm not careful with how I choose to live my life, I can quickly be 50 and still be working a shitty job like this one. This is why I need to get promoted. But Uri does not seem to live in sorrow. He's joyful, sings when he types a message to a customer, and whistles happily. This demonstration of happiness worries me a bit. No one who's been working for so long in a call centre should be this happy. He's either trying to make us think this isn't as bad as it is so he can lure new colleagues into the trap he fell into, or he's taking antidepressants. Neither is good. As time passes, the second option seems to be the main hypothesis.

I quickly get the ball rolling. I'm a natural. I've been doing this for so long now, it feels like riding a bicycle. I answer stupid questions and take care of meaningless problems while being paid minimum wage by a multimillion-dollar corporation. I don't even bother to try and pretend to be interested in the product. Grey offers a €50 voucher which we can use on their website to shop any item we like.

'This is our welcoming gift!' they say.

The average cost of a single item is more than €100, so the voucher can get me a pair of socks if they're on sale.

The one thing that stands out to me in this job is how easy it is to issue refunds. In my previous jobs, we would only give refunds on very specific occasions, but here, it seems like we just give money away. In one day, we can give more money in refunds than we receive at the end of the month on our paycheck. Most of the customers order clothes online and contact our support to tell us they have never received their goods. We can 100% say that they did because we track the deliveries. Grey does not care; they prefer to give the money back. Uri tells us about this, and he's getting angry when customers are demanding a refund. He knows they know that they can ask for one because that policy has been put in place for so long that customers know about it just as much as we do, even though it is supposed to be internal information. He grunts when he processes it, even though the company wants us to do it. Who are we to deny the customer's rights, especially when encouraged by our employer?

This job is also the one where I receive the most insults. Whether by phone or via chat. People feel comfortable talking down to me and being rude. They're demanding, so don't hesitate to insult me before I can even start saying hello. They know we're obliged to refund them. I have almost no way to fight back. The company's quality standards once again restrain me, and I can only endure and receive the attacks without fighting back. How much more will I take? This can't be healthy in the long run. I've had a pretty long run myself, and I'm becoming emotionally numb. If I could at least fire back, that would give me some satisfaction. But all I can do is politely warn them that if they insult me two more times, I will end the chat. After the first warning, they usually threaten to kill me if I don't refund them.

Grey operates a lot via chat. To protect our secret identity, much like Elastigirl and Mr. Incredible, we have to choose a fake name or an alias to communicate with customers. When initiating a chat, the customer will have an option to input a name so we know who we're talking to. On their end, they will see our chosen name, usually a generic one, for example, *Thomas*. This is to avoid any customer tracking us. A name is enough information to find someone on social media, especially when agents share their profession. If I'm talking to a 'Thomas' and they're working for Grey, it won't take long until I can find their profile picture, hobbies and address. This causes a variety of issues, especially for women, once again. Some customers (although I don't want to generalise, mostly men) think being nice over the phone is an open window to a potential relationship with a female agent. They spend hours searching the Internet to find the name of the agent they just spoke to. As a result, we're no longer allowed to disclose where we're working from, what our real name is, or any information that could lead to customers finding us. It's important to keep in mind that these policies were put in place after incidents happened, meaning that some people found women working in customer support in another country simply by using their name.

Like salt and sugar, Grey and I don't mix well. I usually get to enjoy a few weeks at work before realising my job is only going to bring me despair and sorrow. Grey has the nice distinction of being straightforward with me and showing me its true colours from day one. I instantly hate it here. I get insulted on a daily basis, and I started the job only a few days ago. I give a lot of money to customers who use the most absurd excuses to get refunds from me. I send out my salary several times a day. I'm being underpaid to be taken for an idiot 8 hours a day. I knew this job would only be temporary, but I didn't think it would be this short. I checked my personal emails and saw that another company had replied to my job applications. I did a background check on that one as well, and I learned that it is just as bad as Grey's. I'm drowning anyway. I might as well jump from one sinking boat to another. Maybe it'll give me a bit more time to hold on to life a little bit more.

My manager wants to meet with me. I jump on the call. He's nice. He introduces himself and asks if I like the job. I tell him that I'm quitting. He feigns sadness.

'Is it because of the salary?' he asks.

—'Yep'.

He knows. We all know. I'm not paid enough to endure this much abuse. At least give me a better paycheck if you want me to go through this. I put all the equipment back in the box I kept, knowing I shouldn't throw it away for this reason. I send it back within a week, and I make room for the new box which should arrive soon.

Chapter 6: Green

The equipment box for Green never arrived. They messed up with the delivery and as a result, I don't have a work computer for my first day. I have to use my personal laptop, which isn't bad all things considered, cause I can stay in bed during the training.

This company, Green, specialises in car rental. My mission, if I accept it, is to take phone calls from customers who want to book a car with us. It's a different form of support because I assist people in making purchases. Because of my young age, I have a hard time understanding how anyone can book a car over the phone rather than on the Internet. I want to see the car I'm about to rent in a picture before placing the booking. That might be due to the fact that I'm not able to picture any car from any given name mentally, but the fact remains that these types of bookings are made a lot more easily on the Internet. And as if that wasn't challenging enough already, this is topped by the worst booking system ever made in the history of booking companies. This company uses a system so old that it might've been around when they did the calculus to land on the moon for the first time. Not only did this company provide no computer for the job, but they're also expecting me to work on this Windows 98 software to take bookings. It looks like when a PC crashes and reboots instantly. Because it was overheating or because there's been a power shortage for a brief second. In the first few seconds, when the PC powers up, there's a black screen with white text on it saying 'Rebooting' or something like that. This. This is it. It also looks like the invite command window on Windows. This is what we have to work with. We're basically given a scenario in 18 steps in which we have to type in several commands to make a booking on the back end.

It starts like this: 'Would you like an automatic or a manual?'. If the customer wants a manual, we type in Z//A. For an automatic, we type in Z//X. These are logical and easy to remember.

Question 2 is, 'Do you need three doors or five doors?' For three doors, we type Z//dnumt. For five doors, we type Z//dnumf. I'm almost sure I could've guessed it on my own.

The farce continues with 16 other questions we ask, each of them having a command associated with the response given by the customer that we should type into the system to make the booking. After the final question, we enter yet another Latin formula into this archaic software, and we're given a price for the booking. We will announce this price to the customer and ask them if they take it. I don't know what happens if they decide not to take it. Do we hang up the call or try another round of computer scrabble to see if the price will decrease by switching from an automatic to a manual? It goes without saying that we have to do the 18 steps all over again. My two weeks of training for this job were the most chaotic I've ever had. The training is done via WhatsApp because the company did not send me a computer to work on and because I'm too lazy to install Zoom on my own computer. Each morning, the trainer calls me and puts me on speaker. He's in an office in Dublin, training another Spanish girl and me. He's Spanish himself, so they're often flirting with each other while I'm on the other end of the line, regretting to have learned Spanish in high school. All we do, from 8 a.m. to 5 p.m., is the scenario. He asks me for the 18 questions we should ask a customer, and I answer them with the commands we should type into the system. Every time we finish, we start over with new answers. This time, he asks for five doors with a kid's seat. This sounds boring, but being forced to do it for 40 hours a week does more than bore me. It is to the point of mental exhaustion. I know the formulas by heart and do not want to know them. My body physically rejects the learning process, but my mind has somehow printed all of it because of how repetitive it is. The trainer does not seem to get tired of it. He still has the same enthusiasm each time we have to make a pretend phone call. He sounds like a man who's trying to imitate a monkey to make children laugh. I'm not sure why he feels the need to disguise his voice this way, but I don't have enough energy to react. The whole booking process is draining everything out of me, and there is no humanity left in me to laugh or be desperate. I let the trainer know that I won't finish the training and end the call. I don't bother informing the recruiter or my manager. I never even met the manager.

I just need this to end at once. I'm closing my laptop, and I take a nap. I'm already in bed, so that's really convenient.

Chapter 7: Pink

I sent a bunch of applications to a bunch of companies. The last two have been awful, but I did try to apply to world-renowned companies. One in particular is called Pink. They're one of the biggest resellers in the world and are looking for support agents to assist big sellers on their platforms. I found the ad interesting because, for once, I wouldn't be dealing with customers but with sellers. This sort of gives me the illusion that I'm progressing on my corporate path since I'm switching to the other side of the fence where people are probably a lot more civil. I also find hope again. The lay-off in Yellow was a small bump on the road, and I can now get back on track with my corporate goals.

Pink contacts me and says they're interested in my profile. Finally, something good happens. The recruitment process takes a few months, and I have to do several interviews for it. It's not normally the case, so I'm inclined to believe that the position has more value than a regular one at Grey. Even though I'm desperate for this job, I play it cool and pretend like I'm not. I don't want them to sense my desperation. They need to believe that I'm a trophy they need to work hard to get. After all, my resume is full of big company names already. I'm quite the woman for the job.

I ended up getting the job, and I'm being given my starting date. I'm told I will be receiving my working computer on the same day. Why I'm not receiving my machine a day before is beyond me, as a late delivery could mess up the beginning of my training. But I will blame it on my newly acquired anxiety thanks to the corporate world. I wait patiently for the computer to arrive, and it does. I checked the package and made sure I had everything I needed to set up my PC correctly. I find out I'm missing something. It's a security key. It works like a USB key, except it holds encrypted codes that are used to authenticate me so I can use the company's systems. Without this key, I'm able to attend the meetings, but I can't do anything else. I will notify the person in charge once I get to meet them. I turn on the computer and log on. The PC is nice, brand-new, and the new model of a good brand. There are stickers on the screen, which I'm satisfied to take off to baptise my new working companion. I'm receiving an invitation to a meeting, and thanks to the steps I was given on a paper in the delivery box, I can join my first meeting to meet all my colleagues and the trainer. The trainer is a young Spanish woman in her 30s, and she seems nice.

She's announcing that the training for this job will be six weeks long. This is by far the longest training I've ever had, and it's also the most complex. The training begins with a video of the bald CEO in his garden talking about his philosophy of life. This feels a bit like a cult and also ridiculous. Unless this man is about to give me his credit card number, I don't want to hear from him. What good wisdom can come from a man this rich? Is he about to share the secret of happiness with the employees he pays the minimum wage and fires in bulk any time the value of his company's shares drops by 0.01 cents? What a good introduction. The first day is dedicated to the history of the company. Who founded it, when and where. It's the American dream in Kindle format, and we have 4 hours to read it. At the end of the day, our trainer asks if we have any questions or concerns, and this is when I tell her about the security key I'm missing. She says she'll take care of it, and I should be receiving it in the next 48 hours.

The next day, I didn't receive anything. I'm expecting this; after all, I reported my issue at the end of the day, so it's my fault if it's not here with me today. But on the following day, something laughable happens. I received a text saying that my delivery had been completed. I checked my mailbox and didn't see any package left for me. I used the text to contact the delivery company and found out that they sent the security key to one of my friend's house. I'm not sure who messed it up, the company or the delivery agency, but the security key, which holds precious encrypted codes and should only be detained by an employee, ended up being delivered at a friend's house in the city. I was able to connect the dots when I saw the delivery address and when my friend confirmed she had received something that she hadn't ordered.

The people in my training are not comfortable with each other. We don't really connect all that much. One guy messages me, and he asks if we can go on a meeting, just the two of us. I accept. We exchange small talk for a minute until he finally lets it out: he hates the job. He tells me he thinks it's awful, that the trainer is stupid, and that what they're asking us to do is way too much for way too small of a paycheck. There he is — the self-aware employee. There are two types of employees in the corporate world. The self-aware ones, who cannot believe that people would willingly work in such conditions, and the actors, who understood that pretending was key to survive.

My mind wants to scream, 'Thank you! Finally, someone notices as well. I thought I was becoming crazy', but my mouth says otherwise.

I find myself defending the job.

'Maybe it is not as bad as we think', I say.

I'm not convinced by what I'm saying, but I say it anyway. Have I been too formatted by the corporate world that the words coming out of my mouth are all politically correct now? I want to speak ill about this job. I want this guy to know that I agree with him and that he's right. But I can't bring myself to do it. It's like a filter has been applied to my speech to smoothen it. I also can't trust someone I've never met in real life. Who knows if these meetings are recorded? I can't take the risk of being fired already. I need the health insurance. I will be an actor from now on.

We're being shown videos about customer interactions, and one stands out from the rest. It's a video talking about empathy. Empathy seems to be the new sensation in HR offices because it is being shoved down our throats like that chocolate cake in the Matilda movie. The video shows a bear talking to a fox. The fox fell into a hole and can't come out anymore. At first, a deer says, 'That sucks'.

The bear reassures the fox, 'I know how you feel; I've been there'.

That last sentence makes the fox realise that he's not alone and feels a lot better instantly. Our trainer asked us what we thought about the video. There's a small moment of silence. We all look at each other, wondering if we're going to be playing along with it or burst out laughing. We decided to go the corporate way, and one girl said she thought the video was interesting, which speaks volumes about human interaction.

'Exactly!' says the trainer.

She insists that empathy is super important and wants us to understand that this video is a perfect example of dealing with a customer. I'm uncomfortably swallowing my laugh because it seems like we're all going to pretend like these 2 minutes of animals talking were a life-changing experience. I nod yes, and I unmute myself to agree with the last comment. Once again, this is not what I want to say, and even less what I think. I feel insulted that such an easy metaphor is being used before we're asked if we understand it. I believe we all had to pass 1st grade to get the job, so I'd say we're good at understanding animal representation. But I also can't stop wondering if this is a joke or not. Does the company believe that we're so stupid we need a video of animals to know how to handle human interaction? Or do they treat us like idiots in an obvious way so we doubt our own intellectual capacities and don't question anything that comes after that? There are many ways to teach a lesson to an employee, but a childish animation isn't the one I prefer. The video has probably been projected at the same seminar in which Yellow's quality agents learned about the concept of empathy. Pink's trainers must've been there and thought the idea was brilliant. Once again, the decision to include this video in our training session has been taken by the manager of a manager of a manager of a manager. They will always be told that their decision was genius since no one else at their level will contradict them and because we agents at the bottom of the pyramid aren't giving honest feedback either. If I could, I would probably ask why the bear didn't give the fox a ladder to get out of the hole.

The concept of empathy is all the rage nowadays. Customer support agents must show empathy when interacting with customers, especially when denying requests. My personal theory is that a director, who's eight ranks above mine, must have seen the satisfaction rates going down and had to act in consequence. The idea of showing empathy to a customer is as stupid as offering a band-aid to someone who just broke their arm. If a customer is angry, it is because the outcome of their case resolution isn't the one they were hoping for. If I can't refund a customer, it is because the company's guidelines state that I should not be refunding this customer. By simply offering empathy, Pink expects me to calm their customers who are mad because of the guidelines that they set and that only they can change. The same way that bear did to that fox. This simple act of kindness that I learned on a Tuesday morning, in a 2-minute video, is supposed to calm the customers and increase our satisfaction scores to satisfy the gods in heaven.

When I finally start to handle real cases, I find myself lost. The training focused heavily on theory but didn't have any practice. I had never seen what our system looked like before starting taking my first email. A lot is going on on the screen. There's a lot of information to fill up and many boxes to tick, and I'm not familiar with anything. I wasn't given any processes to follow or any indications on how to find them.

Handling cases in Pink is much more complex than anything I've done before. The documentation of our cases is a lot more precise and also really confusing. Each case needs to have a category and a subcategory to be classified properly, and I'm given no indication on how to properly tag a case. The drop-down list shown on the screen is so long it does not fit on the screen. If I take too long to classify my case, I will be reprimanded. If I classify it wrong, I will be reprimanded. I have to choose randomly and in a hurry, to comply with the time constraints. Each time I classify a case wrong, I get a warning. I always classify it wrong because of how complex their system is. Each call I get feels like a fever dream. Each email I receive feels like an enigma. I have no idea what everyone is talking about. It feels important. It sounds serious. But it's nothing I can wrap my head around. I'm unfamiliar with the terms these people use. I'm also not keen on the language we use internally. It usually gets better after a few weeks, but in Pink, it does not. The issues I'm confronted with are like none of the previous ones. It's also often the results of our system and algorithm acting out at random without an explanation. Prices drop, and items are being withdrawn from sales. There's no known reason for any of these situations, not that I know of. Whoever coded the website to act this way must know, but I don't know who that is. Also, the poor sellers who have to deal with the repercussions of such acts can only get me on the phone to ask for clarification. I'm just as in the dark as them. I don't think I should be the one in charge here. The sellers I get on the phone generate millions of profits each year; their issues are serious. They should be talking to someone who can better their situations, provide solutions or at least clarify what's going on. Is Pink aware that I'm not prepared at all? Do they know their training and system are too complex for the human brain? Do they care?

A lot of the time, the tools we need to use are not working. There's an error on the website, or we don't have the permissions required to access the tool. We need to report this as a ticket to the engineering team, which is an even more complex task than using the tool itself. The link to create a report isn't given to anyone, and the information requested in the form is confusing and uses verbiage I'm not used to. I often randomly fill up the blanks, hoping for the best. A lot of time can pass before getting a reply from the technicians. Weeks, months, sometimes years. I need access to these tools to solve my cases, so it obviously affects my productivity. It's quite common for the technicians to come back to me only to inform me that my submission wasn't filled out properly and they won't be assisting with my request as long as it is not right. They also don't give me an indication of how to correctly fill out their form. I have to submit a ticket once again, not knowing if it is going to be enough this time.

The schedule I have to follow is wild, to say the least. I have to get up before sunrise. Stay awake until late at night sometimes. Weekends and bank holidays are always days I have work. The recruiter asked me if I was OK with it during the interview. I said I didn't mind, even though I absolutely do. The phone lines aren't open during the early hours of the morning, so I'm not sure why they insist on having me online. Emails can most definitely wait. The rooster I'm following changes a lot each week. This directly impacts my social life and my ability to hang out with my colleagues outside of work. It also prevents my body from getting used to a routine. I'm not able to sign up for any physical activities like a salsa class on a Thursday since I can sometimes work on a Thursday and sometimes not. If I start the day early, I finish with no energy or will to do anything else. If I start late, I wake up late because I finished late the day before as well, and I don't have time to venture out of the house before the new shift starts. I work like a machine once again. My body is tired, and so is my mind.

I meet my manager, Helena. Upon joining the meeting, I saw her fully dressed in black. She looks like she's coming from a funeral. A fashion funeral. She has a sense of style unlike any I've seen before. She has many tattoos, piercings, and hair that would make a Hollywood star jealous. I tell her that her style reminds me of a witch. She genuinely feels positively touched by that comment. She smiles. Her managing style is closer to Damiano's rather than Doris's. Thank God. I can barely get in touch with her, though, as she's somehow more overworked than I am. But it's nice to know that we won't be a burden to each other, at least.

Like in Blue, I have to click on a button to receive an email in Pink. There's always an email waiting for me. In the middle of a case handling, I can receive a phone call, disrupting my ongoing thought process to worsen my attention deficit. Juggling with two balls isn't impressive enough for the circus manager, and Pink decides to make us work even harder. They implemented the chat functionality and told us that in a month's time, we would also receive chats on top of calls and emails. These contact types will not be prioritised in any way. I can receive a chat in the middle of replying to an email, just like I can receive a call. Usually, companies have dedicated schedules to have agents on the phone line and other agents on the chat line, but Pink really wants us to become the performers of the month with obviously no salary increase for this new workload. In fact, we're supposed to be getting shares in the company after a certain period of time working for them. This is what my contract stipulated when I signed it. In a change of heart, Pink decided to give me a minuscule salary raise instead and cancelled the idea of giving me shares. Essentially, my salary is a tiny bit higher, but I'm the one losing in the exchange since shares are worth more than a few euros added to my payslip. Pink announces this as good news, and I would almost be happy if I wasn't stupid. In the end, this is a disguised budget cut, and the raise I should be getting for the extra amount of work I'm given is only another ruse to give me less money than I was originally entitled to. I now have to deal with the stress of two different live contacts, which can occur at any given time. I'm also receiving my first chat two weeks after the announcement Pink made about introducing chats. Originally, a month was supposed to pass before receiving our first chats. This is earlier than we were told, and I was not given a heads-up that this could happen. I find myself having to deal with a new communication canal I need to be trained for and wasn't ready to use.

Pink often debates whether or not we should be saying the word 'Sorry'. Saying sorry means we acknowledge that we are wrong, which does not sit well with Pink. For a while, they forbade us from saying it. Instead, we have to use empathy statements. The decisions are taken by a team a lot higher on the hierarchy scale and sometimes months before agents are informed. The ban on the word 'Sorry' was decided a month ago, and some of us are still using it. We're being reprimanded when we find out that we should remove that word from our professional vocabulary, even though no one has informed us that we should. After two months of keeping our lips sealed, we are told we should be saying sorry again.

Networking is an important part of the corporate world. This is how people get their name out there, to be noticed and remembered when a professional opportunity arises. A lot of my teammates are bowing down to higher-ups like they were Beyoncé herself. They send many positive messages and encouragement and rejoice when the company reports great numbers. This is ass-licking at its finest. The saddest part is that no one actually cares. I haven't seen anyone behaving similarly getting a promotion that way. I also can't really understand why anyone would willingly be happy for their corporate employer to make millions while being underpaid and overworked. All of this is for the sake of networking. This goes beyond the scope of work, too. These people share news on LinkedIn and proudly comment on the company's posts with ridiculously positive messages. I'm getting nauseous reading them. The lack of sincerity is beyond me, and even if being a hypocrite is a requirement to remain employed, I don't see myself pursuing the act outside of my working hours and outside of my working platforms.

This creates an environment of distrust. Seeing colleagues worship Pink makes me question their intentions and how much I can confide in them. Sometimes they ask, say in the work group chat:

'I didn't have a call for the last hour. Is it the same for everyone?'

Perhaps it is a coincidence. Perhaps no one is calling right now. Perhaps their computer has a problem. Whatever it is, I do not want to comment. I don't want them to know if I'm working or not. They don't have to know. If I admit that I didn't receive a call all morning, what are they going to do with this information? Report me for lack of productivity? Or are they genuinely curious? I can't tell. The way they act throws me off guard, and I keep everything to myself. This should also be my manager's concern only. I feel bad for her, though, cause she has to manage a team that gets larger by the day. She does not have time to focus on one person, let alone the 30 employees she was assigned. I can barely get in touch with her. Pink is scheduling meeting after meeting with her, and it's a mystery to me what these reunions are about. Managing a team requires a minimum of interactions with us, but here, there aren't any. It's not her fault either; this is how her schedule is set. As a result, we're being left alone without a manager most of the time. We have no one to turn to when issues are occurring. I need to figure out who to contact for payslip problems or who to turn to request new equipment. I'm in the woods by myself.

I found out that I had to fill out some sheets in Excel for the job and submit them to an internal system for customers. The format and content of these sheets must be precise, or the system won't accept the file I'm submitting. The system often denies my files but never indicates why. I'm getting an error, and it's up to me to determine what's wrong with my Excel sheet. Just like the rest, I was never told how to do that. I wasn't even aware that I would have to use Excel. I put on my resume that I could perfectly use Excel, but this was obviously a lie. I'm sure I'm not the only one who put 'Excel' as one of my skills on my resume because I didn't know what else to put. I could've said I make a great lasagna. It wouldn't have got me the job, but at least it wouldn't have been a lie. I have to face the consequences of my actions, and I have to make the file work. I'm confronted with a list of numbers, characters and formulas that my brain cannot decipher. They're like hieroglyphs to me. I ask for help from my colleagues, and most of them don't know how to help; they're stuck in the same situation. Only a handful of them can help, but they're busy, and I feel bad asking for help on the same issue over and over again. This could be easily solved if the company made us take a one-hour training class to learn how to format the file properly. But this is one hour less in production time. Pink prefers to provide poor assistance rather than no assistance at all. I'm grateful they're not an airline company. It would be dangerous having pilots not briefed on their destination. They're just told to fly but not told where to.

There is one person in my team who saves me regularly. Her name is Marisa, and she's Italian like me. She knows so much about everything: how to fix the Excel files or what to do in any given situation. I messaged her at first because I didn't know who else to turn to. Now I know that if I'm drowning, she'll be the hand I can reach for. I see her every week during our team meetings. She uses this time to pass on knowledge to the team out of the kindness of her heart. I usually use team meetings as a platform to do comedy and jokes. Both are useful for the team. We sometimes get agents from other teams in our meetings. One quality agent joined our meeting one day, and she wanted to talk about the stupid new guidelines she had just come up with. After a few minutes, she turns off her webcam and leaves the meeting abruptly. We don't really understand what's going on. She writes a message an hour later saying she started crying out of nowhere and needed a moment to recollect herself. I'm not even surprised at this point. I always knew we all needed therapy.

After a day of work, my mind goes blank. I cannot tell a single thing I remember doing. I genuinely could not tell anyone, even if they pointed a gun at me, what I was doing during my day. I try, at night, to think strongly about the 8 hours that just passed. I remember two phone calls, one about a package being the wrong size and one about the price of an item significantly dropping without the consent of the seller. Put together, this is probably 30 minutes of my working day. And this is all I can think of. I spend 40 hours a week taking phone calls and emails about various issues, and I don't have anything to pull out of my brain when I try to recollect memories. I wonder if it's because I am making things up on the spot every day, making it impossible for me to remember all the nonsense that comes out of my mouth just to get through the day. I know that I'm clueless most of the time. Most of the issues I am getting confronted with seem too important to be handled by me, and I know that I'm trying to search for the camera as they do in 'The Office' because this has to be a prank. The worst part is that the people contacting me about their issues are big sellers. Big companies making TVs, makeup, food or clothing. We're talking about millions of euros worth of products, and the issues they have need to be solved by me. These are the most responsibilities I've ever had, and I was unprepared to deal with them. Jobs are on the line, deadlines are to be met, and the consequences for messing up are real. This is no longer about video games or hotel bookings. Still, it's just as mentally draining as any other support agent position. I feel empty inside, and I can't remember the last time I processed a thought.

Like in my previous jobs, I can seek help when I need to. Requesting assistance is a tough task, almost harder than dealing with a query I can't resolve. I have to fill out a form with ten sections, one of which is a section asking for the research I've done before initiating contact with the helpers. The scenario we want to avoid at all costs is the one where the helpers will point out a paragraph of a page in which the information I'm looking for is located. A basic 'duh, it's right here' moment. I can accept this rhetoric if I ask my mom, 'Where are my socks?' and she says, 'Did you check under your bed?'. I'm having a harder time with the company sweet-talking me into believing I'm an idiot. I can read. I know about the control +F search function. If I can find the answer to my query without contacting my unhelpful colleagues, I absolutely would. As colleagues, we're supposed to have each other's backs. If they are where they are today, they've been where I was before. They did support as well. They should be used to repeating the same thing over and over again all day, like they did before, like I still do. Many of them rephrase my questions. I'm not sure they're understanding the issue either. I can't tell if we're both in the same boat or if they just don't want to help. I'm usually rephrasing queries to users when I don't understand their issue either; this buys me time. It's funny to see someone else using the tactics I use to take people for idiots. Unfortunately for me, their souls evaded their bodies just like any senior corporate employee. Our interactions aren't nice. So, there has not been a lot of change since the Blue Days. It's nice to see that the non-team work ethic carries from company to company. A small portion of their team is made of genuinely nice and helpful people, which I'm always hoping to get picked up by when asking for help. This is like playing Russian roulette with my mental health. It makes me wonder if they're nicer because they've been working in this position for less time than the others. Maybe disdain for colleagues grows over time, and their own isn't quite ripe just yet.

The systems we're using in Pink are so complicated that I'm not sure the programmers even understand what they made. There are probably 20 tabs I need to have open all the time on my browser because I constantly need to check them for various reasons. For example, if a product is taken out of the website, one seller will contact me to know why. Yes, we do pull out some products without notifying the sellers and without giving them a reason. There are 13 systems, each located on a different internal website, to determine the reason why an item has been removed from our website. The first one gives me five different identification codes for the same item. I must use some codes on some systems. For example, code one can be used on systems 2, 4 and 8. Having a centralised system was apparently not on their to-do list. The system two tells me if the item's price corresponds to the current market. If not, the seller needs to lower their price: that's the reason I have to give them. There's also no way to contest or reverse it. The third system checks our warehouse availability, and the fourth checks if the items are stored in the right place (for example, fireworks can't be stored too close to flammable items). The seventh system checks if any EU non-approved ingredient is contained within the product and if it can be consumed. Writing this list in my notes makes me yawn again. I have to document each step I take during these cases. I'm tired of writing about this, and I can only imagine what it feels like to read it. I feel sorry for the quality agents for once. For hundreds of people in Pink, this is the day-to-day job. And when we have to do this during a phone call, we feel absolute ecstasy. The seller's tone shifts to 'impatiently angry' while I'm only at the 6th check, mixing up codes. I'm surprised that operating this way is considered an accepted business practice. I would be fuming if I were the seller on the line. Are my products no longer being sold? And no one tells me why. This would make me furious. And I'm only the messenger on the other side of the line who can't do anything about it. Surprisingly, none of these sellers are yelling at me. They expect an answer but are professional and cordial. Of course, they're in charge of sales, and we're one of the biggest retailers in the world. I suspect they're afraid of wronging us. They need Pink to survive, but Pink does not need them. This creates an unfair balance in our partnership and gives agents like me immunity in terms of verbal outrage. I don't think I ever had an unpleasant call.

Working from home is a luxury I can no longer live without. It's part of my routine, and it's convenient; I wouldn't change it for anything in this world, except maybe pizza. In an effort to reunite employees with the office, Pink organised a pizza day. The deal is this one: if we work in the office that day, they'll give us free pizza. Because I'm an easy fish to bait, I agree and prepare myself for the longest working day to come. I start my shift at 8 a.m. Usually, waking up at 7:50 a.m. when working from home; I wake up at 6 a.m. that day. I need an hour to have breakfast and prepare and another hour to take the bus and go to the office. During the drive, I wondered if the people around me did this daily. This is exhausting. I arrive at the office, and I'm given access to my floor, where I meet all my colleagues for the first time. It's always a weird experience to have the people I used to see on a screen for months in front of me. It's like meeting an actor who plays a character I like on a TV Show, minus the excitement. I chose an empty desk to set up my working laptop, and I started my day. In an hour, I do more than I would do in 2 at home. Nothing distracts me, and I can't take any breaks since my manager is a few feet away from me. After finishing all my work, I stare at my laptop, not knowing what to do. If I were home, that would be my cue to start a laundry machine. But I'm in the office. I can't do my chores on my working hours right now. I look at my colleagues; I think we're all pretending to look busy. This is the first hour only; there are eight left. This day will never end. After what felt like an eternity, we're finally given our short 30-minute lunch break to enjoy our hard-earned pizza. The multi-million dollar company generously offers two kinds of pizza: plain cheese and pepperoni. Not contempt to choose the two cheapest pizzas a pizzeria can offer, they also made sure to pick the most low-cost they could find. Delicious Neapolitan pizzas are being made in this city every day, but the frozen dough and American cheese prevailed over the centuries of Italian gastronomy. My Italian colleagues and myself are outraged. This ploy to lure us into the office was just another disappointment, and the only reason I'm here in the first place turns out not to be valid after all. To add insult to injury, I still have 4 hours left to work and an hour of traffic to be stuck in after that.

The disastrous culinary experience at least brought one positive change to my working life: I'm now acquainted with my teammates. We exchanged our phone numbers during the lunch break, and we talked a little bit. Personally, I feel like I am only really bonding with Marisa. She's the only one cynical enough for me to trust, and she also saves my ass several times a day.

Pink comes up with more corporate-friendly ways to reunite the team and organises a night out at a famous pub in Dublin. Since most of my colleagues are twice my age, I hesitate. I talked to Marisa and asked her if she was planning on going. She says she does because Pink will pay for the drinks. My mind is set as well. I will drink to forget that I work for Pink, at Pink's expense. I understand that the company privatised the first floor of the pub for us, so upon arriving, I gave my name to the doorman, and he let me in. I feel like I just walked in a laboratory where a virus turned everyone into a zombie. The room is filled with people who are each in their own corner. The centre of the pub is relatively empty. I try to interact with as many people as I can. They're all quick to start work-related conversations. In less than five minutes, I learned that one of my colleagues drinks one bottle of vodka by himself each week to cope with the job. Another one confesses she has nocturnal terrors and can't sleep at night. She says she hears the sound of the ringtone regularly in her head. The next topic that is brought up is how difficult it is to classify a case. I decide to walk away from these conversations to protect what's left of my sanity. I sat next to Marisa, who understood that we should avoid people as much as we could. I spend the night with her, watching my 40-year-old alcoholic colleagues make out with one another in the middle of the pub where no one else stands. Everyone drinks litres of alcohol. It is uncomfortable for me to be confronted with the damage of this job once again. I made a lot of effort not to go into that rabbit hole, and I'm now seeing that all my colleagues are deeply mentally affected. Marisa and I decided to finish one cocktail and leave. The room is filled with despair, and it's contagious. It's one thing to be miserable for eight hours a day; I'm not going to do overtime at the pub.

I have reached my one-year anniversary with the company. This is a big milestone. I'm passing probation and getting my first raise. My weekly meeting to go over my performance is not held by my manager, Helena, this time but by her manager, Samuel. He greets me and introduces himself. I know who he is. I mean, I heard of who he is, but it's the first time we're talking. He asks me how I'm doing and tries to make small talk to make me comfortable. He re-centres the conversation and congratulates me on the anniversary. He told me that this was the first step to achieve before becoming someone in this company. He winks. The meeting ends. I'm speechless. This is what I've always wanted, and yet I didn't get any satisfaction from this call. I did not believe a single word that came out of his mouth. *Becoming someone.* What does that mean? I'm not no one because I don't have a manager status. And what should I become? A depressed nerve wrack like the quality girl who lost it in our meeting once? This conversation was supposed to be a tap on the shoulder and an encouragement message, but it had the opposite effect. I was not seduced by the idea of climbing ladders anymore. When I work so much, I don't see how quickly time passes. It's been a year already. I didn't take the time to think about what it meant. Samuel told me that it was the first step in leading me on a successful path, but I believe it was the first dig to make my own grave. I have no skills that are useful to the company. The only reason why I didn't get fired already is because I'm entertaining the whole team during meetings. I'm unaware of most of the processes we need to follow to fix issues I'm still unfamiliar with. If I'm chosen to be promoted, why aren't my colleagues, too? Marisa is the one colleague who helped me get through the day here. I message her at least twice a day to ask her to rescue me. And she so kindly does. She knows everything. And in detail. She can resolve any problem. She even trains other colleagues and me on issues she learned how to fix on her own. And she does that willingly, without a salary bonus. In fact, she has been doing that for two years now and is sometimes being asked to train recruits for a whole week on complex topics no one else knows how to handle. The problem is that training people is a profession in itself: trainer. This position is better paid and no longer includes the duty to deal with customers. Marisa asked several times to be promoted since she was already doing the job but without a pay raise. The answer was always the same:

'We're not hiring at the moment', 'There are no roles to be filled for this position'.

If there are no roles to fill, why can't they find a trainer to train their employees and have to ask her? If she can't get the promotion, I will not either. This meeting with Samuel acted like an electroshock: he was creating hope. The hope of a better life that would never become a reality. I'm going to get old and dusty if I don't get myself out of here. I'm sensing a trick, and I do not like it. I'm looking for another job and find one; I'm quitting the following week.

Chapter 8: Brown

I stumbled upon the advertisement for this job and thought it would be my next one. The company specialises in data storage and is also one of its leaders in the market. It is still customer support, but this time, it is Tier 2. Tier 2 would only get cases that first went through regular agents before being escalated to them. This is because some issues, like important money sums, are too delicate to be handled by first-line support agents. They can also be too complex (big technical problems). It gives me the illusion that I am moving forward in my corporate career since, after years of regular support, I would now be moving on to a higher role. The working days are from Monday to Friday and the hours are fixed. No more weekend shifts, and no more having to wake up at 6 in the morning to write stupid emails. And the cherry on top: there are no phone calls. This department does not take any calls and only operates via email. I am seduced by the idea of complete silence after years of being traumatised by ringtones. The catch is that I will be hired by a contractor, not the company itself. The difference with Blue, however, is that this contractor will handle my contract only, not my daily tasks. They won't have any involvement in the job itself, which reassures me. They won't be the middleman between an exigent company and an overworked capitalist slave. Being employed that way, though, has its cons. The contract is fixed. It is a six-month-long contract which can be renewed for another six months and so on until I reach the length of 23 months. On that 23rd month, my contract will not get renewed, no matter how good of an employee I am. A quick Google search teaches me that the reason behind this is that on their 24th month of employment, employees can ask for a permanent position, have access to better benefits, and, in the event of a lay-off, get greatly compensated. Keeping a contract under that 23-month period ensures that employees remain disposable and won't cost anything when the time comes to get rid of them. This type of contract is also put in place as a loophole to avoid giving a salary raise for longevity. The promise of a weekly job with no phone calls does win the long debate I have with myself on whether or not I should apply. I am mentally gone from my previous job, and whatever this one is, it can't be worse than what I've already done. I get to work. I am hyped for this position and put my heart and soul into the application process. I created a brand-new resume and made sure to include all the big company names I worked for and now despise. It got the recruiter's attention. He came back to me the next to tell me I wouldn't be a good fit for the company. *What?* That is the first time I have ever gotten a 'no'. I am not used to it. Customer support jobs aren't supposed to be difficult to get; this almost feels like an insult. I checked the feedback the recruiter left for me. It says that my resume does not look professional enough to pass the first round of interviews. I take a moment to stare at my resume like I would stare at a Van Gogh painting in Amsterdam. For once, I have to agree with the enemy. I put purple neon lights on a black background. Of course, this isn't professional. I'm not sure what I was thinking. I've been collecting all these jobs without breaking a sweat. Improving my resume is a noble ambition, but it must be done correctly. I worked on a second version, which is a lot more corporate-friendly, and sent it to the recruiter, asking if he would accept this one. By a fortunate series of events, he does. I passed the first round of interviews, and I am now scheduled to meet three different managers, one after the other. Each meeting lasts 30 minutes, making the interview last a total of 1 hour and 30 minutes non-stop. This is the longest and most difficult interview I've ever had. I prepared two days for it. I have notes. I did some research about the company and prepared some questions so they would know I had a look at their boring LinkedIn account. They seem to like me. They tell me that if I keep up with this attitude, I can get another position in the company within six months. This makes my eyes water. Finally, the moment I've been waiting for. This is it. Brown is the company which is going to change my career. The interview is a tedious process, but it pays off: I sign the contract at the end of the week, and I am ready to start a new chapter. Like all of their peers, this company isn't able to take care of the very simple task of delivering a computer to my house. They send it off to a supermarket 1 hour away from my house. As a result, I miss my first day. I am given a bunch of documentation to review and catch up on. I am done within three days, though I was given two weeks to do this. One of the documents I have, directs me to that stupid empathy video. I stare at the void, wondering what I'm doing with my life. I mostly read through the long PDFs I was sent without giving it too much thought. I know all of this information will not be retained, and I prefer to spare myself a headache when possible. I quickly find myself wondering if I should be doing anything else. I'm not being contacted by anyone, a manager or a colleague. I have no meetings scheduled and no directions as to what I should be starting to do. The training for this job is like none I've seen: there is no training. This is comical since I'm supposed to be an advanced agent. I don't know anything about the product I'm supposed to offer support on, let alone on the level of Tier 2 agent. After three weeks, my manager finally contacted me for the first time. He says I'm going to be meeting with another agent. This agent will be providing training on a specific area: payments. During the first meeting, I learned everything. The agent showed me how to initiate refunds, and I will have to stick to doing that for a while since she does not know how to do anything else herself.

The lack of organisation in this company baffles me. The training was a shit show, but the rest of the job is identical. I was not given any targets or any indication of how to do anything. I'm not sure what I should be doing, for how long and how. I'm also unsure if I should ask. Maybe it is expected of me to know these things because I'm now tier 2. I don't dare to ask. I also did not connect with my manager. My manager, Liam, is hired externally, just like I am. It took me a while before I figured out he was completely useless. He is the equivalent of an amateur sports commentator. Once every two months (if I'm lucky), he meets with me to discuss my performance despite having no knowledge of my actual work. The more I meet with him, the more obvious it becomes. He wants to talk about something else; he makes small talk to make the 15 minutes we have together go faster. Because I want to evolve in the company, I report my progress to him, including ideas I have and projects I am working on. And then, one day, I realised I might as well be talking to a wall. This guy is an external manager, so at best, a supervisor who reports to an actual contracted manager who's ten ranks below someone who could potentially help my career. My efforts are pointless and unseen. And yet, I keep the show going. I decided to break tradition and try with all my might to get a permanent contract at Brown so that I could live happily for the rest of my life.

Because of the mess the training was, it was not hard to step in and offer my help to the managers to handle it. I schedule it, meet with trainers and trainees, create forms for feedback, and support docs for reference. I even train myself on topics no one knows about to become a valuable asset. I train several agents in the same week on different queues while working several queues simultaneously. It does not stop here; I make official resources for agents to rely on, initiate changes in the process, and become self-taught in many areas. I pass on my knowledge to the rest of my team. I give 110% of myself daily, hoping it will get me somewhere.

Hoping that the manager of a manager of a manager will one day see my name and be impressed by my performance. I hope they will free me from customer support and promote me to HR or quality or any of these lazy jobs. Like an elf receiving a piece of clothing, I would be free.

The workplace is drastically different from any previous I've had. Every day, I log into my computer, and I do not say hi to anyone. No one interacts in the global group chat, and I know very few colleagues. I can spend weeks without exchanging with anyone, and my manager does not check on me either. He messages me when he needs something to get done. In my everlasting quest to find a better place for myself, I always accept. But that's as far as it goes. This job is lonely. I don't especially mind since, after all, tranquillity was my main wish. But I do find it careless not to ensure a minimum of group cohesion. Had this been my first job in Ireland, my life would've turned out a lot different. I need my colleagues to rely on me; I need to vomit my disdain for the company while someone holds my hair. In Brown, I don't have any of that. I did meet with a couple of colleagues, but the connection isn't there. We don't trust each other. Because it is so easy to loathe around all day, I think we're all a bit suspicious of one another and are too anxious to admit that we sometimes aren't working when we should be. I can sense that underlying tension whenever I meet a colleague from Brown. We beat around the bush but never addressed the elephant in the room. It's fine, I suppose. I don't need to have new best friends for each new job I start. And if that means not having to witness another company party where everyone makes out and gets drunk, I'm fine with that, too. But if there's one thing I find lacking in this one, it's the camaraderie. In an attempt to get our team to mingle, our managers decided to schedule a team meeting each Friday, which is not work-related. We talk about upcoming releases of cinema movies and new TV shows on streaming platforms. It feels forced. I try my best to say as much as I can each time because the awkward silence of 30 people with their webcam turned on is too heavy for me to handle. I usually overshare and regret it afterwards. As long as I'm not confronted with 10 minutes of silence, I'm OK. I feel an incredibly uncomfortable warmth when Liam asks what everyone's plan for the weekend is, and no one answers. I can't tell if no one has a social life or if they all planned on doing cocaine in a pub's toilet at 1 a.m. on a Saturday. The less we know, the better.

The deal when I got hired for this job was that I would be operating as a Tier 2 agent in several queues. A queue is a place where specific cases are being sent depending on which topic they're related to. For example, there is a queue for payments, in which I will be finding cases related to payments, refunds, taxes, etc. There are many queues, from technical issues to account security. As I'm starting this job, I'm being prepared to deal with payments mostly. But as time passes, I'm getting to know the other queues. This is done by scheduling meetings with colleagues already working these queues and telling me everything they know. It's everything they learned by themselves or with previous colleagues who did the same. Usually, an agent would be performing in one or two queues maximum. For unclear reasons, the people who started with me and myself are expected to work all these queues at once, with the terrible teaching Brown has to offer. Being a Tier 2 agent means being an expert in a specific area. If all areas need to be perfectly mastered by me in a few months while being vaguely told how to solve a 10th of each case within a queue, I will be, at best, mediocre if half of these queues. Most agents tell me to cherry-pick my cases since they don't know how to deal with the rest of them, and no one else in the company has the knowledge to train us. One of the queues is actually only worked by an agent in the US who can meet with us two hours a week. This complicates learning as we forget what we learn from one week to the next. I don't learn enough in two hours to take on cases on my own to get some practice. Another queue has no qualified agent working on it. No one in the company has any knowledge about that queue, so we're unable to learn anything from anyone to become the experts we're meant to be. The learning process has also become a lot more complicated than it should be since our managers forget to schedule meetings and are not keeping track of our progress. It's bizarre. They expect us to be fully ready after a one-hour 'lesson, and yet when they see that no work has been completed because of our lack of knowledge, they do not care. They're not coming after us. And I don't think they have to. Half of the people who started the job with me already quit.

After a few months at the company, I was kind of moved to a new team. At first, I was told that I was only 'backup' for this team and that I would be called upon when needed. They need an extra hand with work sometimes. I am conflicted. It's not a promotion; I'm not getting a raise, and I'm also operating in many departments already. Adding another one seems like an exaggeration, but since the expectations of my managers are so low, I accept in the hopes that they keep me in mind for future and better positions. The new department is support for a service which they just purchased. It specialises in data sharing and analytics. I follow the same training as the other recruits, who are going to be working in this department full time, unlike me. The training is once again done by a not-so-volunteer colleague who shows us her day-to-day tasks while we take notes so we can reproduce them. Over the course of the next weeks, I work more and more in this department. It was supposed to be one in many for me, but my managers fully moved me to this department. I'm not sure if it's because they realised that I couldn't and wasn't operating correctly in all the departments. Or maybe they needed a new employee and didn't want to go through the recruiting process all over again. In any case, I become a full-time agent for this product and no longer take care of the other queues. This feels liberating. Focusing only on one product makes my life easier, and I enjoy working for the first time. I've been pretending to do most of my tasks so far and didn't get anything done. Now, I can specialise in a single product and become a real advanced agent.

I'm being introduced to my new team. It's made of 2 sub-teams, one of which I already know. They're my colleagues from Ireland, and I trained with them. The other part of the team is from the US, and they have a title that we don't have: The Advanced team. I'm confused as to why they would have that title and not us, but it becomes obvious as the days pass. Without being warned, I was back to being a Tier 1 agent. I was not receiving the cases escalated by previous agents; I was once again escalating them to a higher tier. Once again, I am the first line of contact for customers. I am receiving everything, from bug reports to spam emails sent by robots. I applied to be a Tier 2 agent, and I have downgraded to Tier 1 yet again, having to deal with minimal issues. The illusion of any progress I've made professionally fades as I return to doing what I've been doing for the last couple of years. The US team is in charge. It's an unwritten rule, but every decision must go through them. They're not our managers, but they're the only ones who know the product, so their word is sacred. This gives them an unfair advantage as they can cherry-pick their tasks and leave us the most tedious ones. For example, bank disputes and chargebacks. This is one task I find myself having to do despite not having received any relevant training from the Advanced team. It has been decided that they won't be doing them and that the Irish team will take care of it. I have to study the processes closely and on my own to understand how to reply to banks about disputed charges, which are sometimes worth a few thousand. This sounds like a serious deal to me, but neither the managers nor the Advanced team cared to walk me through it. They simply expect it to be done. The other difference between the Americans and us

Irish workers is the contract we have. Their contract is permanent. They are getting paid much more than us, and they're nearly untouchable. Several times a week, they notify our team (through the public channel we use for communication) that they will not be working that day. The reasons vary: they have a headache, they have to update their computer for 4 hours, or there's a tornado in the US. It becomes obvious that none of these reasons are monitored or verified as they simply announce it publicly instead of notifying their manager to take their day off. They can end their working day one hour after starting and face no consequences. My colleagues and I, under the same shady contract, can't take a sick day without a doctor's note. Of course, I don't go to the doctor for a headache, so I never call sick at work, even if I'm not in the best shape. I show up and do what I can because I know that if I call sick, I won't get paid. My American peers, who are doing significantly less than me, can do this at will and can go on about their day. This progressively creates a wedge between the two teams since one has privileges and the other doesn't.

We're a month away from Christmas. I decided to celebrate by going on a shopping spree and spoiling my family with various Christmas gifts. I opened my emails and saw an invitation to a global meeting. I'm curious as to why we would have a meeting with all the employees, as it never happened before. The invitation came from HR, which is not a good sign. I talked with my colleagues, and they believe that this is a bad omen. I'm not sleeping properly. When the day comes, I join the meeting. We're all here, and most of us don't have our webcam turned on. The HR person comes in and announces that the company has decided to let go of its employees in Ireland due to financial reasons. Contracts will be terminated at the end of December. I'm so confused. HR continues.

'I will be sending invitations to some of you for another meeting. If you receive one, it means your contract is coming to an end. If you don't receive one, you will still be employed by the company.'

It is sadism at its finest. Reuniting all the employees, only to tell them that some of them will be fired, is so twisted. I cannot comprehend why they decided to proceed this way. Wouldn't it be easier to meet with the affected employees directly? We're all looking at each other, wondering who will make it out alive. I feel like this is the *Hunger Games*, and I don't know when my time will come. I visibly look anxious. A close colleague asks if I'm OK. In reality, I am thinking about the amount of money I just spent on Christmas gifts, and I can't afford to lose my job right now. HR comically finishes his PowerPoint with the fade-in transitions and ends the meeting since no one dares to speak up after this bomb was dropped on us. The next fifteen minutes are some of the longest of my life. I wait to receive an email. If the email contains a meeting invitation, I'm fired. If the email says I'm safe, I'm not losing my job. The Russian roulette. So many thoughts go through my head. If I lose my job now, how am

I going to pay rent next month? My heater is on every day. Will I be able to pay my electricity bills? Should I be returning some of these gifts? It's not the *Hunger Games*. It's a horror movie. The potential loss of my job makes me realise how real the financial weight of life is and how I can't keep up with the cost of my existence if I'm to be fired right now. Since I first arrived in Ireland, inflation struck, and not having any income was a Damocles' sword above my head. After what felt like an eternity, I received an email: I'm not affected by the lay-off. I can breathe again. I can have a normal Christmas after all. But most of my colleagues can't. We have 40 agents working in Ireland, and 30 of them have been fired. Some of them have children, and I'm not sure if they'll get gifts from Santa Claus this year. I'm also not sure how they're expected to pay for their electricity bills now. One of my colleagues, Pete, whom I was getting along with, was only a few years away from retirement. I can't imagine how difficult it will be to find something else at his age. There isn't a best month to fire employees, but there definitely is a worst one. The announcement ruined the festivities, and 30 people working hard for a company are being let go. The contract states that only a month's notice has to be given, and of course, without compensation (we're all under the 23-month frame). Brown will find new employees to hire in Greece, where the workforce is considerably cheaper than in Ireland. They say it is all in the name of budgetary decisions because of inflation. Brown revenues last year were above a billion and increased by nearly 7% compared to the previous year.

There is nothing worse than customers reporting bugs. And I really mean nothing. When a customer has a problem that I can fix, I can do it pretty quickly, and the case can be solved. If it's something that I cannot resolve, I can also decline the request rapidly and get on with my day. But when someone reports something which should be working and does not work, I know I'm in for a long and unpleasant ride. A typical scenario would be that the customer reports that the page does not actually zoom in upon clicking on the 'Zoom' button. Quite straightforward. I can try on my end to see if it works or not for me, and if it does not, I have to escalate this in the form of a complex report, which takes me one hour to file. First, I have to send the customer basic troubleshooting steps, such as trying another browser, testing another connection, etc. If nothing helps resolve the issue, I'm starting to gather information for my report. This technical report is a page long but requests extensive information about the customer, the issue, and the support case I have. I'm supposed to include every single piece of information known to mankind about this person. I have to summarise the issue in one sentence, and in the next field, I have to describe it in detail. The details I must include should also come in the form of screenshots and screen recordings from the user and myself. Comes in my favourite part: a detailed timeline of the events. This is by far the most ridiculous field from this report, and usually goes like this:

'Jul 25th, 4:56 p.m. GMT+1: User is reporting this issue

Jul 25th, 5:02 p.m. GMT +1: I'm now reporting this to you.'

I have to include timestamps and details of our interactions, even though I'm linking my case, which includes timestamps and the interactions themselves. I'm also being asked if I'm able to replicate this issue on my end, what I tried to do to resolve it, etc.

I understand why these reports should be as complete as possible; I just deplored them. Filing a report is a lot of backtracking, copy-pasting, and a plain-out boring task which can take up to an hour to complete. To add insult to injury, I have to create a report for each customer experiencing a problem. That is, even if two or more customers face the same issue. Suppose three customers are all experiencing the case example issue of the zoom button. In that case, I have to create three different reports that require me to go through each interaction I ever had with all 3 of them and detail them with timestamps. This is extremely time-consuming and not enjoyable. I don't understand why our manager's guidelines make us do this, and every time I try to raise the concern and advise that we could just add a second report as a comment on the first one, I am dismissed. I'm being told that we can't know for certain that the two issues are the same, even though they are. My two eyes, which no one trusts in this zombified world, can tell. The worst of the worst is when all the reports I open for the same issue are being closed as 'duplicates' because they are, in fact, shockingly the same issue. It means I lost several hours of my week to make pointless reports that I knew would be useless. If I don't do them, the engineers will not leave me alone until I do. In a nutshell, I have no choice but to do this, and my voice is not important enough to reason anyone with decision power.

I will say, though, that men in their 40s who are tech-savvy LOVED this. Asking for a screen recording of what they're seeing on their end stimulated them in a way I didn't know was possible. They must think that we're asking them to hand over their research like NASA would ask the calculus of a math genius for their next rocket launch. They must believe that this is a bonding experience between their own humble mind and the talented engineers of this multi-million dollar company. They have no idea it's a ruse to discourage them with the insane amounts of details we're asking for, hoping they would flat-out give up on the idea that this has to be fixed. All so that engineers won't have to work during their 7th coffee break of the day. These men are glad to do it. They are happy to send us their screen recording and recording they did. They send in these 10-minute-long videos where they describe the problem in detail, showing every single piece of information imaginable, including the browser they're using, the date and hour, their location... By the end of the video, I feel like I know these guys. They're like the cool uncles I never had. Seeing people getting involved in a minor issue with such excitement is heartwarming. And they're not even getting paid to do this! As a bonus, most of them include a little bubble in the corner of their recording in which I can see their face, recorded by their webcam. These guys are also sending their own reactions that they filmed at the same time they're doing the video. This is awesome. It feels like a YouTube video at this point. They're making jokes, thinking out loud, talking to themselves, asking questions and then answering them immediately. They even break the 4th wall by looking straight at the camera and talking to me. And I'm the only person who gets to enjoy this little gem of an mp4? This is too good. I'm greedy for more. I usually save those cases for the end of my day when I get to enjoy this little streaming session with popcorn.

Once I get these recordings, I will attach them to my report, and I send this to the technical team. The report gets triaged by another one of my colleagues, the point of contact of the engineering team. She's in charge of sorting out all the reports and deciding which ones are going to be prioritised. The most important ones would be the ones that affect a large number of users or the ones that affect our high-paying customers. If a customer is subscribed to our cheapest plan and their issue only affects them, typically, it wouldn't be resolved, or it could be resolved after a few months (sometimes years). This POC reviews my report and has me send several questions to the user, all perplexing. I can't prove it, but I would bet money on the fact that this person has a secret alliance with the technicians. Most customers usually get scared when we send back many confusing probing questions. When she sends me the list of queries to forward to the customer, she knows very well that this is too demanding for a customer to answer on their own and in their free time. Most customers would not care to have something as silly as a zoom button being fixed. Not if it meant that they had to spend an afternoon trying out all the recommended steps provided by our support team. As a result, my emails containing these questions are often not replied to. My case closes automatically, and consequently, the technical reports I made do, too. These reports never even reached the technical team. Hours of my time were lost to accomplish nothing, all because of the unreasonable demands of this **POC**. Some customers do come back to me and ask if I'm serious. If I really expect them to provide me with so much information and have them try dozens of complex troubleshooting steps.

'I understand this is a lot, but we need this information to continue our investigation.' This is my answer.

Of course, I would prefer to tell them that I know it looks like we're making fun of them because, in reality, we are. But my hands are tied, and I have to oblige to continue this endless circle of keeping technicians out of business because studying Java was tedious enough; we're not going to make them actually work. For ten issues I report, I'd say two get fixed. And I can't speak about the timeframes here.

Some do take a week, while others take several months to fix. Again, this depends on the urgency of the situation. Less urgent problems, which affect a single and not spendthrift enough user, would sometimes not be solved at all. If a technician is in a good mood, they might look into their report and do something about it. However, since the reports are being sorted by order of importance, it is likely that minor incidents would be received months after originally being reported. There hasn't been any communication between our support and the customer since their first message. If a technician receives a report from February only in August, they can and sometimes will close it. I have been asked to close my case 'quietly', which means I have to mark a case as 'done' in a special way so that the customer isn't informed that their case was closed. They also don't receive a satisfaction survey when I do this. The reason is that the technicians decided that it had been too long since this issue was reported. Since the customer did not ask for any updates in the most recent weeks, they probably forgot that they even reported this in the first place. So now we're not only insulting my work and the time I spent filing their endless report, but we're also insulting the customer's efforts to provide all the necessary information and screenshots they so kindly provided at OUR request. I try to object. I'm trying to remember what I applied for this job to begin with. Well, I applied for the money. But really, I should be doing this job because I love helping people and want their issues fixed. I protest and voice out my opinion. This customer has been waiting for nearly six months for someone to fix their issue, and now that a technician has finally picked up their case, we should close it instead of investigating it. This feels wrong, even for the heartless banshee I became after years of doing this. I'm told that I'm not given a choice here. The technician is not going to do anything for the customer. I ask what I should do if they come back to ask for updates. They tell me I should create a new report.

My colleagues and I are part of the support team. This means we offer support to most customers. However, some companies are such important clients that they will get an 'account manager'. Because these companies are paying a lot more than regular customers, they would get a designated point of contact who would offer support instead of us, regular agents. That is how it should work on paper. In reality, these account managers are paid nearly six figures to be the most inefficient beings on the planet. Every time a managed company needs assistance, the account manager will loop us in so we can fix the problem for them. Either because they don't know how to fix it or because they're too lazy. Support agents, though, usually cannot solve these issues. The reason why an account manager has been appointed to these companies in the first place is because they have to receive fast, efficient and, more importantly, specific support, which we can't provide. The huge sums of money these companies are paying are so important that they shouldn't be handled by our support team but by our sales team. And the funny part is that account managers are the sales team. So, in a weird time-space paradox that only occurs in Brown, sales employees will ask support agents to fix sales issues on their behalf while sharpening virtual pencils to look busy. It seems completely normal to the sales team, as I previously contacted their manager to ask what's what. I have been left on read several times. They don't bother to pretend to care.

In an even better plot twist, sometimes account managers simply disappear. They go extinct, like the dodo bird before them. If an account manager is being transferred from one department to another or simply leaves the company, the enterprises are left without the one point of contact they had with Brown. As a kind gesture and demonstration of our professionalism and care for these people, we do not notify them that they're being deprived of one of the expensive features they're specifically paying for. This leaves room for an extremely awkward and unpleasant conversation between these companies and our support team when they find out that no one is managing them anymore. I also did not mention it before, but the exact same thing happened in Pink. Our support team has to deliver the news that no one is looking after them and, in fact, probably hasn't for a few months already. We can try to reach out to the sales department to appoint a new manager, but this is a lengthy, complicated process that can only be done on a platform we have limited access to and no knowledge of. We also have to do this several times since we're often ignored. Ultimately, we find ourselves in a position where we're being asked to do someone else's job, which we can't do. I know there are a lot of hierarchical levels between the CEO of Brown and me, but I do believe I have a better understanding of how to treat customers.

Against all odds, I'm still eager to make a name in the company. After all, I'm one of the only people who seem to be working around here. Or, at the very least, I'm one of the last people to care. I'm observing the methods of my colleagues every day, the colleagues who are evolving and getting promoted. They're always nice to everyone, especially in public group chats. They always make sure that good deeds are visible to the rest of us, much like these YouTubers who film themselves giving food to the homeless. I slowly started to do the same; I replied to questions in public channels, offered to assist my colleagues in their cases, and gave out steps to follow in public, not in private messages, as I did before. To really get my popularity going, I need to aim big. I have to do something that's going to last for years to come so I can become a point of reference. After some brainstorming, the idea comes to me. I'm going to create resources. These confusing help articles all agents use to solve their case: I'm going to create one. All the ones I use always have the name of the agent who created it at the very top of the page. I want to be one of them. I study all the contacts coming through: I take notes of the ones I can solve using existing documentation and those I can't. I quickly realised which areas lacked resources and worked on them for a couple of weeks. I first start with a draft, then a more elaborated version. I added screenshots, schemas, a glossary, and points to remember. After a while, I got a final version I was proud to submit to the product team. I have to explain the purpose of my work and why I want it published at the internal documentation centre of Brown. The process takes weeks. I get notified for every update: the team is reviewing it and adding some corrections. Until one day, my article goes live, and I can finally enjoy all the hard work I've put in and see my name in the Hall of Fame. I open the page in a new tab. I have butterflies in my stomach; I'm excited. This is a big milestone, and I can definitely use it to my advantage in an interview one day. I start to read the article. When I check the name next to the creator, I see that someone else's name is there and not mine. I'm confused. My colleagues all have articles with their names on it. Why isn't mine here? I'm infuriated.

Not everyone is being treated fairly. Hard-working employees will take on projects and additional tasks. They are usually the ones who will be held accountable for their mistakes, too. On the other hand, employees who are known to be lazy will be left alone cause there's no point in talking to them anyway. The more I care about a corporation, the more it will be used against me. If a company sees an employee like me who's willing to do the job of 2 people for the salary of one, they will never reward me with a promotion. They will keep me where I am for as long as I mentally can. It's the best deal they can get: a cheap employee who asks for more when they're already overworked. The most chilled ones who do the bare minimum have more time to network and crawl their way up, while I will be looking at each and every one of them getting the job I think I deserve. At this point, I'm not sure who's the idiot. The company, the other employees, or myself. There's no meritocracy in the field, only the illusion of it to keep me running in the hamster wheel, letting them milk me until I dry up.

I have a history of finding a job and then quitting it when it starts ruining my life a little too much. Though I always have a good reason to resign, I decided that it would be different this time. Brown's contract is the first one with a designated period. It's going to be 23 months, not a single one more. During the interview, I was told that if I played my cards right, I could get a permanent role in a better department. I strongly believed that this was my chance to end the cycle of my misery. I won't have to go through interview processes again. I want a permanent contract with this company because it is the most bearable one I've been in.

And so, I set my plan into motion. I did the most I could to show myself out there and made it obvious that I was in for the long run. I did overtime, I took on projects and initiatives, and I said yes to everything. I helped my colleagues as much as I could, and I kept the meetings alive. If this was a circus performance, I'd probably be breathing fire while juggling five knives and riding a unicycle. I was devoted to the task. I didn't give it my all; I gave more than that. I exceeded my targets, doing double what I was being asked.

There was one area in which I was particularly excelling, and it's one area that has been left abandoned by the team. There were tasks which needed to be dealt with that no one knew how to do. Because of that, a backlog built up, and it kept on getting worse. I took it upon myself to teach myself how to do the job, single-handedly crushed the backlog, created documentation for my colleagues to be prepared for the future and kept on doing these tasks by myself for a year. I did the math one day to see how much money I helped Brown save. It was a five-figure number. This is how much I was able to save the company with my actions. I am proud of that number. I'm sending my report to my managers to find out if they're aware of it or if they care. I'm told it's a good call out, and the conversation ends here. I don't get my congratulations message on the public channel like every other dumb announcement, and the report starts to become dusty, as it will never be open again.

In my dreams, this was going to be noticed. They'd open up a department just for me, thanking me for all the labour and the money I made them earn. These tasks are money-related, and doing them saves Brown a lot of money. My contract is almost up, and I discussed with my manager the possibility of me staying or getting renewed. She says that's not possible and briefly thanks me for all my hard work. Ouch.

We're jumping into a team meeting and a few weeks away from my final day of that 23rd month. My manager says she's currently in the process of hiring someone else, someone who would be exclusively handling the tasks I just referred to. I look at my own webcam reflection in the meeting to make sure I look just as confused as I am on the inside. I wonder if this is the *Truman's show* and I'm being pranked. They're creating a department to handle the tasks I've been doing for a year by myself. No one knew how to deal with these tasks before I got involved. This also means that whoever is going to be hired will be using my own documentation and my work to be trained, I assume, on their own, just reading it. The manager points out how difficult it is to find the right profile for the role. If only there were someone who knew how to do the job and who was already performing sensationally well. If only that person were right in front of them. Trying to make my case is pointless. They won't extend my contract because they don't want to pay me more than what they're giving me right now. I don't even try to say that I'm interested; I don't beg them to reconsider it; I just give up. I do give up. That's the moment when I realised that the corporate world isn't for me. I thought there would be some meritocracy, that my hard work would pay and get me places like all the managers I've had promised. But it didn't happen. It didn't happen in Blue, or Yellow, or Pink, or Brown. I don't think it happened anywhere. I called my friend Marisa, who wanted to be a trainer at Pink; she still hasn't been promoted. It's been two years since I left, so four years in total that she's been waiting. I called my friends who worked in customer support to talk about their situations. They have either been fired by profitable multimillion-dollar companies for 'economic reasons'. Or they quit protecting their own sanity and change fields completely. That's what I want to do as well. Reflecting on these last years, I don't think I've gained anything valuable from these experiences. I have good company names that I can put on my resume, but the fact remains that I was doing customer support. It is not going to get me any other jobs but customer support again. I was naive to believe that it could jump-start a career, that I could become a video game developer, a business manager or a quality agent. I would've taken the quality position any day. I don't feel like I evolved; I feel like I'm at the starting point again. All that I've been doing was getting repeatedly beaten up by all these corporations. They took everything away from me. My will to work, to do a good job, my own sanity, my peace of mind. I have developed anxiety that I didn't have before. I don't smile as much as I used to at work; I lost my ability to force it. I consider myself lucky that I didn't start drinking or doing drugs. I know a lot of my peers have. These jobs ruin lives. These companies are ruining people's lives. And they're doing fine. There's a whole world separating customer support agents and their employers. They won't hire me to do the job I do so well. They're going to hire someone else so that they don't have to raise my salary by keeping me in the company. This new person will have to teach themselves how to do a job until they're let go again shortly after mastering their skills. Or until the company decides to hire support agents in Athens, Budapest, or wherever the labour is cheaper. Because they can, and they do. And there are no consequences for them.

I worked my ass off for this stupid job and to no avail. It didn't get me more money; it didn't get me recognition. After my contract ends, none of this will matter. I will only be back to square one, having to apply for yet another customer support position to do it all over again.

Chapter 9: Outro

After years of ruining my mental and physical health in front of a computer for 40 hours a week, I decided that it was time to give up on the unrealistic hope that I could one day make a name for myself in a corporation through a customer support position. I believe this myth has been created to keep on getting applications from naive souls like me, who look up to employees with a corporation's success stories. I wonder if these people are actors paid to trick me into selling my soul to these companies.

Each job had its own set of flaws, and none of them allowed me to grow professionally. At times, it was the managers who were holding me down. Other times, it was the contract. There was never a situation in which I could win. The colleagues I met along the way were the only thing keeping me sane. And like most of them already did, it is now my turn to leave this field and start working somewhere else. I know this means that I have to start all over again, probably study and go through harder hiring processes. At the end of the day, if it means that I won't have to do customer support one more day in my life, it'll be worth it. I wanted to get a nice corporate position. Now, I want to run in the opposite direction. Had I stayed longer, I would've become more insane than I am now. All the money I would've made with these promotions would've been spent on alcohol anyway, to forget that I'm working for the devil.

It's time to pack up my things, put them in a box again so that a delivery guy can take them back to Brown. This time I won't leave room for a new box to arrive.

Cher said there is a life after love, I say there is a life after customer support. I actually think my life is starting now. Now that I finally escaped; the literal hell of customer support jobs.

Chez le même éditeur

1. *La Chine de Xi : une société modèle ?* – Edel Secondat

2. *Halte mortelle sur le loch Fiag.* - Anthony Claye Mansart

3. *Comment gagner 100 000 euro par an.* - Robin Dubois

4. *Poésie Tang: Nouvelle traduction rimée de quarante quatrains de l'époque Tang*

5. *L'économie à l'envers : Et si le problème était la solution ?*- François Vatin

213

Si ce livre vous a plu, rendez-vous sur le site pour retrouver les livres du même auteur :

https://editionscambli.com/

N'hésitez pas à nous laisser un commentaire sur le site du vendeur.

Pour signaler coquilles et problèmes d'impressions éventuels, contactez la maison à l'adresse :

contact@editionscambli.com